YOUR FIRST BUSINESS PLAN

2nd Edition

Joseph Covello &
Brian Hazelgren

Small Business Sourcebooks

from **Sourcebooks** Inc.

Naperville, Illinois

Published by: **Sourcebooks, Inc.**
P.O. Box 372, Naperville, Illinois, 60566
(708) 961-3900
FAX: 708-961-2168

Cover Design: Wayne Johnson/Dominique Raccah
Interior Design and Production: The Print Group

This publication is designed to provide accurate and authoritative information in regard to the subject matter covered. It is sold with the understanding that the publisher is not engaged in rendering legal, accounting, or other professional service. If legal advice or other expert assistance is required, the services of a competent professional person should be sought.

From a Declaration of Principles Jointly Adopted by a Committee of the
American Bar Association and a Committee of Publishers and Associations

---

The **Small Business Sourcebooks** series is designed to <u>help you</u> <u>teach yourself</u> the business essentials you need to be successful. All books in the series are available for bulk sales. Feel free to call us for information or a catalog. Other books in the series include:
- *How to Market Your Business*   • *Getting Paid In Full*
- *How to Get a Loan or Line of Credit*   • *The Small Business Start-Up Guide*
- *Smart Hiring for Your Business*   • *How to Sharpen Your Competitive Edge*
- *Great Idea! Now What?* • *Protect Your Business*

Library of Congress Cataloging-in-Publication Data

Covello, Joseph A., 1957-
    Your first business plan / Joseph A. Covello & Brian J. Hazelgren. — 2nd ed.
       p. cm. — (Small business sourcebooks)
      ISBN 0-942061-47-0 : $17.95. — ISBN 1-57071-044-9 : $9.95
     1. New business enterprises—Planning. 2. Small business—
Planning. 3. Business planning. 4. Proposal writing in
business. I. Hazelgren, Brian J., 1961-   . II. Title.
III. Series.
HD62.5.C685   1995
658.4'012--dc20
                                                 95-1465
                                                 CIP

Printed and bound in the United States of America.
Hardcover — 10 9 8 7 6 5
Paperback — 10 9 8 7

Contents

Overview

The information in this book is organized in the order of the sequence to be followed in writing your business plan. It includes details on how to research the market, where to find information, what kind of strategies to use, what potential financial resources are available, how the individuals capable of providing those resources will weigh the information you provide, and the importance they will place on certain items of information. You will learn where to be most persuasive and effective in presenting your business plan. For a more comprehensive look at several different business plans, please refer to the companion to this book entitled *The Complete Book of Business Plans* written by the same authors.

NOTE: BECAUSE OF EVER CHANGING FEDERAL, STATE, AND LOCAL LAWS, RULES AND REGULATIONS, PLEASE DOUBLE-CHECK ALL INFORMATION TO ASSURE YOU ARE IN COMPLI-ANCE.

Introduction

If you are a business owner, a business manager, or going into business for the first time, you will at some point need to develop a business plan. Whether you need to raise capital, or to create a clearer focus for your organization, a business plan is as necessary as a road map to a traveler. The path to your final destination has a logical sequence; a good road map will allow you to reach your goal with less hassle and frustration. This book explains essential rules and strategies that you will need in order to develop a simple, yet valuable "road map" to a successful business.

Every business will have differences; but when it comes to establishing a business plan, certain rules and patterns must be followed. This book is a guideline for conducting research, compiling what you have learned, and assembling a comprehensive and thorough business plan.

The situations that arise in business today vary greatly; however, there are key elements that you should be aware of that investors, bankers and other financial sources look for when considering a project for financing. This book explains these key elements and unlocks the door to successfully financing a business.

Although most people associate writing a business plan with raising capital, there are other types of plans that focus specifically on the nature of the growing enterprise. These types of plans are called "strategic business plans" and are generally used and kept within the business. We will discuss these plans as tools for competing in today's tough business climate.

By writing your own business plan, you will be examining, first hand, your business operations and, more importantly, how to possibly improve on them. Over a million businesses are started every year in our country. Unfortunately, only a small number take the time to develop a sound business plan and even fewer will actually follow the steps and strategies outlined in their plan. This book shows you how to take what seems to be an arduous, time consuming, unnecessary task, and turn it into an exciting, rewarding and profitable exercise.

Each chapter explains a component of a business plan. The last chapter is a sample business plan for you to refer to as you read the book. We hope this will help you in gaining a clearer understanding of what your own business plan should look like.

Whenever you take a trip to an unknown or unfamiliar place, you should carry a map with you. Businesses also have unfamiliar and unknown terrain. If you are writing a business plan for the first time or the tenth time, this book will guide you through the important sequences and steps in a simple and highly effective manner, and get you the results that will allow you to compete in any business climate.

Chapter One

Powerful Guidelines to Writing Your First Business Plan

When it comes to writing a business plan, most people think it's about as much fun as taking a trip to the dentist. They usually focus on the pain, rather than the results. Let's face it, writing a good business plan will take time, patience, a lot of thinking, hours of research, and hours of writing and editing. But think of the results. You will know your business better, and be better assured that it will flourish. In addition, you will have a better chance of obtaining financing. Most importantly, you will know how to conduct business and compete at a more sophisticated level. The time invested in developing a business plan can make the difference between success or failure.

Consider, also, the edge you will have over your competition. Millions of businesses do not have a business plan. They are simply reacting to the conditions that exist, much like a sailboat on a windless day. The point made here is that when you take the time to fully develop a sound business plan, you will have a greater advantage in maneuvering and changing your course when the climate is not to your benefit.

A Few Facts

About one million new businesses are started each year in America; of those, approximately two hundred thousand will survive five years. This translates into one in five businesses making it to their fifth anniversary. This is an alarming statistic! Why in the world would only one in five businesses in the "Land of Opportunity" survive so short a period of time? There are several reasons; however, the most common happens to be the most controllable. There is no magic equation for success, but one basic rule holds true: "A business owner who fails to plan, plans to fail."

A business plan helps entrepreneurs and business managers to think through their strategies, balance their enthusiasm with facts and recognize their limitations. It will help you avoid potentially disastrous errors like undercapitalizing, creating negative cash flow, hiring the wrong people, selecting the wrong location, and pursuing the wrong market.

A winning business plan requires time: fifty to one-hundred hours to write an effective business plan which would include research, documentation, analysis, and review.

Entrepreneurs should start planning at least six months before they initiate a new business. This takes into consideration the time you need to devote to its "start-up" while working another job. Six months gives you time to sharpen and focus your business ideas, test your assumptions, and improve your management skills.

If you don't want to wait six months, then dig in, and begin your incredible journey. Maybe you are the type of person who can accomplish the following processes in a shorter period of time; however, these essential elements must be part of your task.

Your New Enterprise —Before Start-Up

Decide on your choice of business. This choice will depend on a few important factors:

- How much money do you have to invest?
- Can you attract other investors?
- What return do you expect?

- Where is your expertise?
- What do you like to do most?
- Are you willing to work harder, longer hours?

Often people develop preliminary business plans for a number of different businesses before actually starting their business.

Consider a Start-up's Impact

Before venturing into your "start-up" consider these possibilities. Your income may suffer, your work hours will multiply, and your family relationships may be strained. You will have expended your personal cash, and assumed a debt.

At times you may feel like you're running behind, and you may become more irritable or critical with people around you. You will see less of your friends and family; you may get more headaches, backaches, or stomachaches. You may feel guilty at times when you take time off from work. Your life, for a time, may be "all work and no play."

Don't despair! These feelings and circumstances are a normal part of starting a business, or embarking on a new project. Just don't give up. As Robert Donovan once said, "Giving up is the ultimate tragedy."

HOT INFORMATION SOURCES:

Start your research.

- Your local Chamber of Commerce—they will assist you, whether you are a member or not.
- Trade shows—a one-stop shopping source for businesses, suppliers, and various consultants.
- Trade-association executives—ask them what is hot in the marketplace.
- Trade-magazine editors—Send a press release to as many as possible.
- Local networking meetings—a tremendous source for leads. Start your own if you have to.
- Federal, state, and university programs.
- Your state commissioner of Economic Development.

- S.C.O.R.E. (Service Corps of Retired Executives).

- U.S. Embassy in the country or countries you plan to do business with.

- Businesses in noncompetitive locations. You might want to use a magic phrase such as: "I've got a problem and I think you can help me."

- Foreign Trade Zones Board—this entity is there to review and approve applications to import foreign goods.

- Small Business Administration (SBA).

- Newspaper Editors—send them a press release also.

Define your business. Write a mission statement of fifty words or less that outlines what you will sell and to whom, and what will make your business different (i.e., *Your Unique Selling Advantage*).

Example: To provide useful, applicable solutions to business owners and managers in the areas of marketing, business planning, finance, accounting, and promotion. And, to fully utilize our management teams' experience and knowledge to increase revenues of each of our clients' enterprises and companies.

The Business Plan

Name Your Business

This is a vital decision. Advice: keep the name straightforward and descriptive. Make it as distinctive as possible. Avoid grandiose, overworked adjectives.

Your business name should be like a headline to an article. Describe who you are and what you do in your name, whenever possible. A dangerous marketing tool is to make customers guess what you do. Your competition may already have a descriptive and straightforward name that is attracting your potential customer.

Example: All City Heating & Air Conditioning Company

Select Outside Advisors

You will need a competent attorney, management consultant, accountant, insurance agent, and banker. Also helpful: a marketing consultant—he or she may save you time, money and misspent effort.

Develop Your Business Plan

This is why you purchased this book: to get you started in the right direction. (But wait until you have read all the secrets and critical elements to a winning business plan contained in this system.)

Convince yourself that proper business planning is an absolute necessity. *Your business plan is the heart and soul of your operation and the most important set of documents provided by you to any lending institution or potential investor.* It explains all the financing you need, and most importantly, it will give your financial sources persuasive information about your venture.

Put your business plan to multiple uses. A comprehensive and realistic business plan will help you accomplish many essential objectives, including the following:

1. **Take charge of your entrepreneurial life.** The business plan is evidence of your initiative. It shows that you have the discipline to focus your energies on an important project and understand how to achieve progress and growth, solve problems along the way, and achieve ultimate goals. The business plan is the foundation and pillars of your vision and will allow you to structure your ideas into reality.

2. **Lay out a master blueprint.** The business plan is to the entrepreneur what a set of detailed architectural drawings is to the builder. It determines the details that will be used in reaching your objectives. It shows you the logical progression of steps needed to reach your established goal. It may also help you consider an alternate, and possibly better route. The business plan is a powerful management tool.

3. **Communicate your master plan to members of your team.** The business plan is a concrete statement of purpose which allows you to communicate to your colleagues a step-by-step agenda for reaching your goals. Some portions of the business plan can also be used in training and coordinating meetings, as well as teaching staff persons what their role and accountability will be in making your business function successfully.

4. **Attract money to your project.** Potential suppliers of capital and other needed resources—bankers, brokers, investors, future partners, etc.—will place great value on your business plan as they determine whether or not to participate.

Your ability to create trust and respect can be greatly enhanced through interpersonal contact with these potential suppliers of capital. However, you may not even get a chance to get to know these people on a personal basis; therefore, you must have a professional document to present in written form. Your business plan will be your initial selling tool—"your business resumé"—when attracting lenders to participate with you in your venture.

What Potential Suppliers of Capital Look at First

There are four critical areas of the business plan that investors will consider heavily before they involve themselves in your venture. These areas are:

1. Your Management Team
2. Your Current and Projected Financial Statements
3. Your Products and Services
4. Your Marketing Plan

Make sure that you build a strong case for each of these critical areas.

Management Team

Your *management team is very important.* Potential investment sources place a tremendous amount of importance on the team of managers that will be making crucial day-to-day decisions. The success or failure of your enterprise will depend on the experience, maturity, and common sense of you, your partners, your board of directors, and your management staff.

Any management team needs balance. This balance will give you the ability to provide the organization with four essential elements:

1. Planning
2. Organizing
3. Control
4. Leadership

BALANCE within the management team, as a whole, includes the behavioral, technical, and conceptual skills applicable to the development, production, and delivery of both current and future products and services. At a minimum, the management team must have, or develop, skills in management, marketing, finance, and operations.

The strength of your management team must be diligently articulated in your business plan. A company with a formal structure will greatly enhance its ability to raise capital, and achieve its goals in less time and with far less expense.

Use honesty in the judgment of yourself and each member of the management team. Don't allow yourself to sway from truth or reality. If your management team is weak in any of these areas, you should consider bringing in top-notch, experienced individuals to your board of directors to help you in these areas, as well as for overall inspiration. Outside professionals can offer your enterprise tremendous leverage—without carrying them on your payroll.

If there are responsibilities which cannot be fully covered by your inside management team, evaluate them and contract with consultants and professionals who specialize in these areas. They will assist in your growth and development.

Your Current and Projected Financial Statements

Financial—Present and Future. Determine your cash needs. Project your expenses and review your sales and profit objectives.

> Tip: If you have access to a computer, purchase an inexpensive ($60-$200) business plan organizer. When it comes to the financial section, business plan software will save you time and energy, and it will help you create the use of a cash flow budget by using various reports.

(These reports should compare actual to budgeted income and expenses on a monthly basis.)

You should also prepare a preliminary balance sheet. List your assets and liabilities to create a "snapshot" of what your company looks like at a given moment. Your balance sheet will be a necessary tool for your banker and accountant.

The financial projections that you document in your business plan should be well thought out. Plan on devoting a fair amount of time to their development. If you have to tell the investor to ask your accountant about something regarding your financial position, you project a less-than-solid business to the investor.

To avoid this, include projections on:

1. Your Profit and Loss Statement
2. Your Balance Sheet
3. Your Cash Flow Statement

When calculating your projections for the future, at a minimum, illustrate monthly figures for the first two years and annual projections for years three through five.

Many novices miscalculate the cost of sales. Entrepreneurs are often very concerned with developing the product to fit a projected need in the marketplace, yet sometimes forget to calculate in the cost of the "delivery system." Therefore remember to ask yourself, "What is the total cost of the sale?" or "How much will it cost me to generate these sales?"

Your Products and Services

Your products or services are obviously very important when attracting potential capital sources. Discuss the characteristics of your products and services:

- How do they differ from similar products and services?
- What customer reactions may be anticipated due to these characteristics?
- Explain how you will satisfy customer needs and wants.

Describe any unique value-added characteristics your products and services provide to the customer, and how these will give your company a competitive edge. If your product or service has evolved over the past few years, explain how and why.

Describe how the product works or how the service is used. Will your product save your customers time or money? Will your product or service generate more profits for your customers? If so, how?

Are there any tests or case studies which have been performed that will help you back up your claims? Obtain that vital information and document it in your plan.

What is the product's or service's life cycle? Explain it to the investor. You may even want to create a simple chart covering the life cycles of your products and services. Also include the time factors influencing your ability to make money and the effects of economic cycles.

Typical stages of a product or service life cycle are:

1. Introduction Stage—Intense marketing campaign which introduces a new or unique product or service.

2. Growth Stage—Sales begin and growth occurs.

3. Maturity Stage—The market begins to be saturated with the unique product or service. Competition increases as awareness of product becomes common.

4. Decline Stage—Newer, more unique and more advanced products enter the market. Loyal customers continue to buy your product or service. Not-so-loyals begin to look at alternatives, and eventually may shift their business to the newer items.

Discuss your plans for the next generation of products and services that will be introduced in the near future.

Be prepared to contact several different investment sources and groups to discover which capital sources will be most interested in your particular venture. For example, some suppliers of finances will only look at real estate transactions. Others may only consider franchise concepts, while others may wish to invest in a manufacturing enterprise.

Your Marketing Plan

Your marketing plan is next on the list of importance. This area requires a fair amount of study and analysis on your part. Although it may seem a lengthy task at the onset, you can still have a lot of fun with it. Here is where you find out who is out there, what the competition offers and what they don't offer, whether or not your product or service will outsell the competition, and what Unique Selling Advantage (USA) you will have over your competitors, etc.

You may even discover that the timing is not right for your enterprise and it would be beneficial not to go ahead with your plans. This would not be a negative find. The time and money you would save if you should wait for a better time, or pursue another market, would be invaluable. Your future enterprise may depend on what the market dictates after a carefully designed marketing analysis. So have fun with this section and enjoy seeing what is out there!

Market Analysis describes the existing marketplace in which you plan to operate your business. Key points for defining the market segment for your products and services are:

1. Product features
2. Life-style of your targeted customers
3. Geographical location
4. Cyclical factors

How many competitors share your market? How is the share of the market distributed among the major participants? Is the market growing at a rapid rate? What are the major trends towards the development of the shared marketplace? Summarize your view of the trends and the implied opportunities from your market analysis.

You will want to list the strengths and weaknesses of your product and service. When covering your strengths, you need to be sure to place at least as much emphasis on marketing as on your product, if not more.

List several distinct advantages over the competition in the following areas:

1. Actual performance
2. Quality and reliability
3. Production efficiencies
4. Distribution
5. Pricing
6. Promotion
7. Public image or reputation
8. Business relationships or references

If you know of any weaknesses in your product or service, list those also and show what steps you are taking to alleviate the problem(s).

Developing a marketing strategy is the art and science of planning for and implementing a promotional campaign that will generate sales for your enterprise. Such strategies are to designed to enhance, promote, and support the advantages, features, and benefits of your products and services.

This section should be designed with one word in mind: STRATEGY. When thinking about a strategy, you must take into consideration your business activities, strengths, and direction. What type of strategy would you put together if your very existence depended on it? Your competition becomes the enemy who is bound and determined to see you fall. A good strategy could save you.

Your strategy should be defined in such terms as to capture your share of the market in as little time as possible. With this in mind, how will your customers perceive your company and products, relative to the competition? This is *critical* and worth repeating. How will your customers perceive your company and products, relative to the competition? A good way to find out is to *ask them*. Conduct a market survey. This is an easy and inexpensive way to find out the answer to this important question.

Several other questions to which you should give serious consideration:

- What can be said about your competitors' products or services that will change your customer's minds?

- What is your Unique Selling Advantage?

- What strategies will you use to promote your products and services?

- Will you use television and/or radio?

- Would it benefit you to conduct seminars or participate in trade shows?

- Will you use telemarketing and/or outside sales representatives?

- Do you need to hire a Public Relations Agency?

- Have you considered direct mail?

- Will you use brochures and flyers?

- Will you sell your products and services locally, nationally, and/or internationally?

- What other creative ideas will you come up with to generate leads?

- Are your strategies consistent with your evaluation of the marketplace and your capabilities?

- Have you defined your targeted market into a narrow window, or does your product appeal to a large market?

- Are your strategies based on facts or assumptions?

- Is your appraisal of the competition open-minded and honest?

- Is the expected return on investment sufficient to justify the risks?

- Have you thoroughly examined other strategies that your competitors are using? Could some of their strategies be adapted to your environment?

- Is your strategy legal?

HOT MARKETING TIP

Look at gripes first, then create a marketing strategy. Look at everything about your industry that could frustrate or irritate a potential customer. Ask people what irritates them. Try to internalize the same problems so that you may experience your customer's frustrations. Then, design your marketing strategy (and even refine your product or service) based on your strengths vis-à-vis these issues.

Your Unique Selling Advantage (USA)

It is important to understand how vital it is to adopt your own USA, and implement it from the president through the sales team, and to your clerical staff. Everybody within an organization should have a solid understanding of what sets you apart from the competition.

Your USA is that single, unique advantage, benefit, essence, appeal, or big promise that holds your product or service out to the prospective customer—one that no other competitor offers or advertises. You should be able to articulate, in one or two crisp, clear paragraphs, the Unique Selling Advantage of your business's product or service.

The backbone of your entire business concept, your USA needs serious consideration. You would do well do ponder the following comments:

Your USA is literally the unique advantage that distinguishes your business from that of anyone else. This is a concept that your entire enterprise should be built around.

Without a USA you cannot build a consistent and effective marketing campaign.

Identify the unique advantage(s) that you should build your marketing efforts around. You need to define it in a clear paragraph. Once you have developed your own Unique Selling Advantage, formulating a winning marketing strategy will come much easier. Therefore, tell it accurately and intelligently and be straightforward.

A USA may be that your product is made entirely of all-natural ingredients or has a warranty for double the amount of time of your competitors' warranties. Maybe you offer three times more follow-up in calling, writing to, or actually visiting your customers after they purchase your product or service. Possibly your product is completely hand-made, the only product in your area, and the competition will take years to produce something as good as you offer. Maybe your business stays open two hours longer than all of your competitors' businesses for added convenience to your customers.

You probably get the idea. Go ahead! Create a USA that lets people feel like they cannot live a moment longer without your product or service. You may be surprised how easy this is.

Chapter Two

The First Pages

It is important to note that the format of your business plan, the amount of detail it contains, and the visual presentation may vary according to the intended use and readership. The following summary of the content of the business plan is intended to show you the elements needed to compile a winning plan that will attract potential financial resources, as well as provide valuable information regarding the establishment and/or growth of your venture.

In the rest of the chapter, we cover the items that you should consider including in your business plan.

Cover Sheet

If you are appealing to prospective investors, money brokers, bankers, and venture capitalists, include a cover sheet, preferably on company stationary, displaying company emblems, and logos. This will help place your application in a framework of legitimacy.

Keep your cover sheet as simple as possible. Identify yourself, your business, and the institution or party to which you are addressing your application and include the date the plan is submitted. Here is a checklist of items that may be included:

A. Business information.

1. Name of business

2. Location, address

3. Telephone numbers

4. Contact person(s), including titles.

B. Business paragraph—promotional description of business goals, potential, and outlook.

C. Capital required—current and anticipated future needs.

D. Name(s) of the person(s) recommending you to the investor.

E. Include a paragraph notifying the investor that all information being provided is proprietary and strictly confidential and may not be released without your written authorization.

On the following page we've designed a sample cover sheet as an example.

Table of Contents

This index will not only help your prospective lender to understand the road map you are placing before him, it will also make a statement about you: i.e., you are organized, thorough, sensitive to the needs of those you are approaching, and able to manage the "big picture." Type up the Table of Contents last.

A sample table of contents follows.

Executive Summary

This portion of the business plan must be designed to capture and hold the interest of the party to whom the plan is being presented. It is here that you capture your public's interest— it can make you or break you. Make sure it can be read in a few minutes. Make it sell! Keep it to within two to five typed pages.

This critical executive summary encapsulates the entire business plan in a few paragraphs by giving the most succinct statement possible of the

BUSINESS PLAN FOR:
Home Improvements, Inc.
1234 East Main Street
Suite 1012
Anywhere, Arizona 85999
(602) 555-1919

January 199X

CONTACT:

Michael X. Swann
President

This Business Plan is copy number _____

This Business Plan is confidential and is the proprietary property of Home Improvements, Inc. No reproduction of any sort, or release of this document is permissible without prior written consent of Home Improvements, Inc.

Sample: Cover Sheet

Table of Contents

Sample: Table of Contents

nature and objectives of your business which would involve:

- Its mission
- Its Unique Selling Advantage
- Your projections for the future (sales, costs, and profits)
- Your needs (inventory, land, building, equipment, working capital, and other resources)
- Procedures and timetable for repaying investors
- The capital you are requesting

This summary is a crystallization of the entire business plan in an overview format. Don't neglect this section. It will demonstrate that you can focus with clarity on your goals and state, in no-nonsense fashion, who you are, what you want, and where you are going.

Since the executive summary serves to summarize your whole plan, it is often the *last* section written, after all of the other pieces have been put together. A sample Executive Summary appears on pages 89-92.

Sample: Mission Statement

To provide customers with high-quality exterior aluminum siding and double-pane windows where we can be proud of the integrity and craftsmanship of each product sold to the end-user, and offer superior customer service throughout the warranty phases of the product, remembering that each customer may be a tremendous source of referral business to our company.

Chapter Three

General Company Description

I. The Context of Your Business

This statement will provide a "big picture" perspective of the industry to which your business belongs and prepare the reader to better understand how your business fits into the total picture. It should include:

- Industry background—how big the category is; the different segments; the industry trends.

- Growth potential—In view of the trends described above, provide a statement (in dollars) of the future growth potential of the industry in which you are competing.

- New products and developments—What new developments have arisen in the recent past that will make your product or service more attractive to the consumer?

- Economic trends—evidence that spending trends are favorable to the industry.

- Industry outlook and forecasts—the future of the industry according to industry leaders, experts, economists, government forecasters, and other authoritative sources.

Sample: Business Background

In a published report by the Improved Contracting Unit of Westeck International, the exterior aluminum siding market is growing at a rapid rate. The report claims that, "the market for siding in the United States is virtually untapped. The United States is a very immature market with tremendous growth potential."

Over the past three years, companies have developed and shown that additional features can be provided for this type of industry. These companies have focused on the use of technological advances to steadily improve the quality of aluminum in exterior siding.

These advances and the positive reports made by New Consumer Product Reports, which states that firms selling home value added products will prosper greatly in the coming decade, are encouraging testimony of our future in this area.

II. Profile of Your Business

It is important to remember that throughout your business plan, you must inform the reader of all major factors, positive and negative, that may have an effect on the outcome of your organization. This section should provide the reader with the concept of how your business works and why it has a unique chance to shine in the marketplace. Make sure to ask yourself the following:

- What is the precise nature of your business?

- How have you developed your products and services? Give a brief history.

- What are the economic trends? Give evidence that spending trends are favorable to the industry.

- What is the organizational detail of your business?

- What are the factors that influence your business? Be sure to include local economic factors, seasonality, dependence on special vendors or suppliers.

- What are your plans for research and development? Include:

  1. The nature of your test-marketing procedures

  2. Results achieved

  3. Product development

  4. Legal control of process and/or product.

- Do you have contracts and agreements? Identify here and include copies in the Appendix; for example, resale agreements, service contracts, leases.

- What are your operational procedures?

  1. For ventures involving manufacturing a product, consider:

     a. Physical space requirements

     b. Machinery and equipment

     c. Raw materials

     d. Inventory and supplies

     e. Personnel requirements

     f. Capital estimates

  2. For ventures involving wholesaling and/or retailing, consider:

     a. Physical space requirements

     b. Purchasing procedures and plans

     c. Inventory system

     d. Staff and equipment

     e. Training

     f. Credentials

III. Profile of Your Specific Market

Accurately defining your target market requires much time and effort. In structuring your market profile, make sure you have done your homework and research with great care and due diligence. Don't assume that your target exists and/or that it can be created in a relatively short period of time.

Sample: Current Business Position

Currently the Arizona market distribution is shared by nine participants. Home Improvement, Inc. enjoys a thirty percent share of this market. There are four other major competitors that share approximately sixty percent, and the remaining competitors share a combined total of ten percent of the market.

The stability of this market segment is expected to increase; however, some volatility has been introduced to the market with the current national recession.

Define your specific market:

- State precisely who the consumers of your products or services are.

- Note the geographical scope of your market, including size and population.

- Consider the growth potential of your target market.

- Evaluate your ability to satisfy the market's demands.

- Know how your business plan will enable you to attract new customers while keeping the customers you have.

When developing a profile of your target market, it is important to remember that your research will determine the strength of your analysis. The time you spend on this section should be spent wisely. Your local library and your telephone will be your strongest allies. Use them to their fullest.

Take advantage of the information and statistics already available in books, directories, and case studies. Thorough research will impress potential investors more than you can believe.

Sample: Demographics of target market

HOMEMAKER

Age   35-65

Income . . . .   Fixed

Sex . . . .   Female

Family . . . .   Full nest

Geographic . . . .   Suburban

Occupation . . . .   Homemaker

Attitude . . . .   Security-minded

IV. Anticipated Challenges and Planned Responses

This section of the business plan sets forth your contingency strategies for dealing with anticipated barriers and challenges. These are some of the main types:

A. The Competition Factor—establish for each of your key competitors:

1. The similarities and differences when compared with your business.

2. Their strengths and weaknesses.

3. Your "competitive edge," your Unique Selling Advantage, enabling you to prevail and stay on course.

4. Your insight into how the competition will try to block your market entry and how you will respond.

Sample: Competitive Overview

Competitive threats today come from three primary competitors and three other dealers in Arizona. HII's products perform in virtually all situations in which there is a home or office where siding and windows can be added.

The ability to offer increased "curb appeal" in addition to providing insulation is a unique attraction to a customer.

Our research indicates that the performance of these products are superior to anything else on the market today. In all comparisons, the HII products provide more features and have superior performance than competitive products. A complete technical comparison is available.

B. The Vulnerability Factor—consider:
1. Product obsolescence
2. Cheaper products on the horizon
3. Cyclical trends in the marketplace
4. Possible economic downturn in the future
5. Turnover of key employees
6. Seasonality of your products and services
7. Compensation benefits package to employees

C. The Legal Factors—consider:
1. License requirements that you must satisfy or maintain
2. Restrictions and regulations under which you must operate, given the nature of your business
3. Future changes in legal or governmental policies that may affect your business and how you intend to respond
4. Any governmental agencies with whom you must register

Sample: Potential Vulnerabilities

There are handicaps inherent in the market. The notable market-place disadvantage is the price that the customer is willing to pay for home beauty and energy-efficiency. The average job will cost $13,000 if the entire home is covered with siding and double pane windows. This cost must be justified in the mind of the consumer.

Corporate weaknesses, due in part to present economic factors, include limited sales personnel. However, steps are being taken to alleviate this as healthier economic trends emerge, justifying expansion in this area.

Sample: Legal Issues

Completed tests have shown that HII aluminum siding has been subjected to tests of impact against both hard and soft objects, in accordance with common rules for Product Durability Testing Requirements set forth by U.S. regulations. The test resulted in performance far superior to the minimum required regulations.

D. The Protection Issues—include:

1. Patents, copyrights, trademarks, and other protection procedures

2. Steps to assure business secrets are preserved

If you are a start-up business, or even an established business that has new products, ideas, or technology that will improve someone's standard of living, and you want to place your products on the market, your products should be Patented, or Trademarked, and all your written material should be Copyrighted.

The two basic kinds of patents are *mechanical* and *design*. The distinction between the two is that a mechanical patent is used when the concept involves a new product that operates mechanically and is something no one has ever developed before. A design patent is an improvement to a previously patented product, such that its design makes the existing product better. However, there is the possibility of infringing on the older patent if all you did was change the design, while maintaining the original mechanics.

The automobile industry gives ample examples of both types of patents. Design changes are radical and continuous as the marketplace dictates. Each change in design is design patented and lasts for three years, while mechanical patents last for seventeen years and can be renewed thereafter.

For your protection, we strongly suggest that you seek the council of an attorney who specializes in patents, trademarks, copyrights, and secret formulas.

E. The Key Man Contingency—involves:

1. The depth of your management team
2. Management procedures in place to assure continuity of leadership
3. Plans for responding to the loss of important personnel

Sample: Key Man Contingency

The founders and key managers of HII have combined experiences exceeding twenty-five years in the siding and distribution areas. The strength of the management team stems from the combined expertise in both management and sales areas producing outstanding results over the past year.

The leadership and alignment characteristics of the HII's management team have resulted in broad and flexible goal-setting to meet the ever changing demands of the quickly moving marketplace that requires our products. This is evident when the team responds to situations requiring new and innovative capabilities.

F. Staffing:

1. Personnel needs you anticipate over time, including head count requirements, training, benefits, expansion, and how these needs will be met

2. Policies on minority issues

3. Policies on temporary versus permanent staff

4. Policies on harassment, racism, or prejudices of any kind

It is important to remember that the information covered in this section must demonstrate that you have covered the problem bases and have carefully crafted contingency plans in place. The information will provide your business plan with more credibility than you think. Be practical and reasonable. Show that you have really done your homework.

Sample: Staffing Overview

The HII development team recognizes that additional staff is required to properly support marketing, sales, research and development, and other support functions.

Currently, HII is composed of eight people. Over the next five years, fifty people will be required to meet the demands of the projected market. These staff requirements will include personnel in the following areas:

- Management

- Marketing

- Sales

- Engineering

- Customer Relations

- Administration

- Manufacturing

- Skilled Assembly Labor

Chapter Four

Present Situation

In this section, you should define clearly how you have come to your current position. Identify how your idea was conceived up to your present position.

Explain the current Market Environment. Is it undergoing changes in technology, demographics, competition, customers, financial conditions?

. . . .

. . . .

. . . .

. . . .

What is the present stage of your industry: infancy, intermediate, or mature stage?

. . . .

. . . .

. . . .

Are there factors that could contribute to the growth or decline of your product? Indicate both the weak and strong points here. It will show that you have done your homework.

. . . .

. . . .

. . . .

Where are your products assembled or manufactured?

. . . .

. . . .

. . . .

What is your product's average life cycle?

. . . .

. . . .

. . . .

With regards to Pricing and Profitability, are current prices from suppliers increasing, decreasing, or remaining constant?

. . . .

. . . .

. . . .

Indicate how you plan to make whatever adjustments are necessary to manage these possible changes in prices.

. . . .

. . . .

. . . .

. . . .

How are your current, or potential, customers using your products/services? If your business is a start-up enterprise, how will they use your products/services?

. . . .

. . . .

. . . .

Where will your main distribution center be? Do you have any plans to open other offices and distribution centers? If so, indicate when and where.

. . . .

. . . .

. . . .

Give some additional information about your management team. Are they all in place? Will you need to hire additional managers or consult with outside consultants?

. . . .

. . . .

. . . .

Finally, provide some information about your current Financial Resources:

Current cash available is $XXXX (as of X/X/X)

Current Ratio is: Assets/Liabilities = XX/XX (XX%)

Current Quick Ratio is: $$\frac{CASH + ACCOUNTS\ RECEIVABLE}{CURRENT\ LIABILITIES}$$

Chapter Five

Objectives Section

In this section you will develop short and long term goals. Here is where you need to formulate a vision of where you want to be in a few years. Make sure that you balance enthusiasm with realism. It is a good idea to use "checks and balances" when you visualize your company's progress. In order to achieve your goals, set a few simple objectives for each year, first through fifth.

With these ideas in mind, begin writing down what it is you want to achieve.

Are your long term objectives to stay a one-person shop, or to build a large company with several hundred employees?

. . . .

. . . .

. . . .

Do you want your company to go public and sell its stock?

. . . .

. . . .

. . . .

Do you want to pass the leadership down to your children, grandchildren, or great-grandchildren?

. . . .

. . . .

. . . .

What will you accomplish with the additional capital: open new offices, purchase equipment, hire key personnel, expand your marketing and advertising?

. . . .

. . . .

. . . .

Will you develop a stronger network of suppliers and/or buyers as time goes on? How?

. . . .

. . . .

. . . .

Will you become a manufacturer at any time? When?

. . . .

. . . .

. . . .

Write down what your intermediate goals are.

. . . .

. . . .

. . . .

What profits do you expect to generate in years one through five?

. . . .

. . . .

. . . .

In order for you to achieve your immediate goals, do you have any debts that must be restructured or paid down? Explain why in detail here.

. . . .

. . . .

. . . .

What will be your expected Net Profits after tax from sales each year? Take these Net after tax profits for a period of five years and show the total for that period of time.

. . . .

. . . .

. . . .

Next, indicate Total Sales Revenue for the same period of time.

. . . .

. . . .

. . . .

Finally, write down at least ten objectives or goals that you plan to achieve with your business.

1. . . . .

. . . .

2. ....

   ....

3. ....

   ....

4. ....

   ....

5. ....

   ....

6. ....

   ....

7. ....

   ....

8. ....

   ....

9. ....

   ....

10. ....

   ....

Chapter Six

Product/Service Section

Will your product/service be easily recognizable and understood by *lending* organizations? It is important to identify your product/service clearly and explain all aspects of the purchasing, manufacturing, packaging, and distribution of the product/service.

Potential lenders and investment groups will lend capital only if they have confidence that the business concept has been clearly researched, identified, calculated, and thoroughly thought out.

Product/Service Description

In concise paragraphs, explain all important information regarding your product/service.

. . . .

. . . .

. . . .

. . . .

. . . .

. . . .

. . . .

. . . .

. . . .

. . . .

. . . .

. . . .

Added Value

List and explain all value-added features your product/service has. It is important to state clearly why your product/service is such a great item: What makes it unique? What sets it apart from the competition? Why would a customer buy from you?

. . . .

. . . .

. . . .

. . . .

. . . .

. . . .

. . . .

. . . .

. . . .

Tests/Approvals

List and explain all test ratings, approvals by government regulations, etc., that add substance to your product/service.

. . . .

. . . .

. . . .

. . . .

. . . .

Product/Service Life Cycle

Identify product life, warranty, guaranty, etc., that cover each product/service provided.

. . . .

. . . .

. . . .

. . . .

. . . .

Trademarks/Copyrights

List and describe all trademarks, patents, copyrights and licenses owned or used. Help the lender assess the value of these additional assets.

. . . .

. . . .

. . . .

....

....

....

....

Chapter Seven

Market Analysis

Do Your Homework!

Have you clearly identified your market? It is very important that you show all relevant data which verifies that you have carefully researched the market.

Potential lenders and investment groups must be clearly convinced that the market you have identified is feasible for the distribution of your products and services.

Market Definition

In this section, you will clearly identify your market, including: competitors, market share, potential market share, market stability, market share and growth, and success of product/service in other markets. Include supporting documentation from third-party independent sources, such as: magazine and newspaper articles, books, trade reports, government statistics, and surveys.

As a first step, describe the market. Provide a history, as well as information about the dollar volume involved, any recent trends in the market and an analysis of your current position in the market.

....

....

....

....

....

Strengths and Weaknesses

Identify marketing strengths, such as: sources of advertising and promotion, public awareness and public acceptance.

....

....

....

....

....

Identify market weaknesses, such as: possible lack of public acceptance and per capita income.

....

....

....

....

....

....

Customer Profile

Identify your customers (including the decision maker), their per capita income, age, sex, family, geographic location, occupation, attitude, etc.

What is your customer profile? (Give details on your typical customers.)

Business Customer

Type of business. . . . .

Size of business (Approximate annual revenues) . . . .

Geographical area . . . .

Number of employees. . . . .

Year in business . . . .

Individual Consumer

Age . . . .

Income . . . .

Sex . . . .

Occupation . . . .

Family size . . . .

Culture. . . . .

Education . . . .

Competition

Identify all competitors. Describe your company plan to effectively compete and gain market share. Include strengths and weaknesses of your competitors and demonstrate their specific strategies. Provide charts, graphs, and data to support your claims.

Who is your competition?

A. . . . .

B. . . . .

C. . . . .

D. . . . .

E. . . . .

F. . . . .

G. . . . .

H. . . . .

How is your competition promoting its product or service?

. . . .

. . . .

. . . .

. . . .

. . . .

. . . .

Chapter Eight

Marketing and Sales Strategies

Marketing Plan

We have all seen great businesses, with a superior location and a unique product, go broke and close their doors. In most cases, this tragic problem can be traced to poor marketing and promotion; i.e., the owner of the business did not know how to market his or her products and services.

Many business owners ignore the potential in the effective advertising of their quality product. Small business owners tend to overlook the need for exposure.

Four essential areas to investigate:

1. Publicity
2. Promotion
3. Merchandising
4. Market Research

Each of these four marketing areas is available to you if you are willing to do the investigative ground work.

The first step is to define your market. Who is your targeted audience? Know its inclinations, its needs, its disposition, then gear your product to fit these.

. . . .

. . . .

. . . .

Entrepreneur Magazine gives us good advice in this area: "All you have to do is forget that you are selling your product or service, and put yourself in your customer's place." Also, it suggests that you, "Ask yourself questions, such as:

- Where do I go to buy it?

- What makes me buy it?

- What media do I watch, read, and listen to, that makes me decide to buy?"

Simply put, you must know what media your market draws to.

You must develop a rock-solid marketing plan. Your profits will literally rise or fall on the basis of how well you develop and implement your marketing plan. Here is your chance to show your entrepreneurial exper-tise. Carefully consider the following ideas and strategies and implement each one into your plan:

- Develop marketing strategies by acquiring market information, by implementing feasibility testing, by accessing competitor track records, and by generating insight into the markets future.

- Pricing a product or service is as much a decision based on customer acceptance, as it is on cost. Consumer research and competitor track record and pricing, customer acceptance, etc., should be demonstrated as your basis. In simple terms, "Charge what the market will bear."

- Determine if your product or service is right for your target market and if they are ready to accept it.

- Channels of distribution need to be effectively and efficiently established if you are going to get your products and services out into the market. This includes production, transportation, materials handling and product packaging.

- Promote your product and service to your target market. Include the media you will use to promote your enterprise, related costs, and anticipated benefits.

- Your marketing budget must be realistic and clearly communicated.

- Your timetable needs to be accurate and plausible.

- Warranty and/or guarantee policies need to be defined.

- Professional resources needed to implement your plan require consideration.

- Monitoring the response of the market to your campaign needs to be considered.

- Testing one approach to another will provide direction for future plans.

Selling Tactics

Identify your sales force. Clearly think through the advantages and disadvantages of commissioned versus salaried sales people. You may consider offering a combination of base plus commissions (monthly salary and car allowance), bonuses, and health insurance. Identify all these parameters in this section.

In the initial stages of your business, will you personally need to go out into the market and promote your product/service? What type of training will you offer for sales staff? Identify the need to increase sales staff as part of expansion and analyze the nature of future staffing.

Will you hire only sales people who have a college degree?

. . . .

. . . .

Do your sales personnel need to be licensed by a state regulatory agency?

. . . .

. . . .

. . . .

Will you be selling your products/services through a network of dealers or distributors?

. . . .

. . . .

Will your sales people have protected territories?

. . . .

. . . .

Where are these protected territories?

. . . .

. . . .

Are your pricing policies set to market or industry standards?

. . . .

. . . .

Will your sales people be able to compete with the prices that you have established?

. . . .

. . . .

Your Unique Selling Advantage

Don't forget that your Unique Selling Advantage is what clearly sets you apart from your competitors and attracts consumers.

Will it make their life more comfortable? How?

. . . .

. . . .

Will it save them time or money? How?

. . . .

. . . .

Will you offer more customer service than your competition? If so, how is it superior?

. . . .

. . . .

Will your customers' lifestyle be any different if they purchase your product/service? How?

. . . .

. . . .

Which Professional Organizations do you belong to that will be of value to your customers?

. . . .

. . . .

What are some of your competitors' weaknesses?

. . . .

. . . .

How can you take these and turn them into strengths for your enterprise?

. . . .

. . . .

Establishing Marketing Objectives

Establish Marketing Objectives for your next marketing campaign. To help meet these objectives, four critical goals should be considered:

1. To increase brand awareness by a specific percentage

2. To generate high-quality leads for your sales force

3. To improve the morale of your direct sales force

4. To increase sales by a specific percentage within a certain time frame

Once your marketing campaign is underway, begin tracking results. Conduct a few preliminary studies a few weeks into the campaign to measure the results, but don't expect these results to be final. In most cases, you should give your campaign at least twelve months to realize final results. Your target expectations may be realized sooner, which would be the result of a well-planned and well-executed marketing strategy.

Advertising and Promotion

Develop a realistic budget for advertising by allocating about five percent of expected annual revenues. Include in your advertising campaign a good mixture of promotional matter. If your budget is relatively small ($100 to $200 per month), definitely include business cards, letterhead, envelopes, a brochure, and stamps. These will give your business plenty of exposure if you carefully follow up on literature sent out.

There are many different ways to promote your business without spending a lot of money. Do a little research on the associated costs in your area of the following items:

- Radio advertising on one station during morning drive time hours (6:00—9:00 A.M.).

- The cost of a convention hall, hotel, auditorium, gymnasium, classroom, library, etc., that holds 30-50 people for a potential seminar.

- How much would a live-remote radio campaign cost? This type of investment will bring you hundreds, if not thousands, of customers within a six hour time frame, which would justify the cost. The broadcast from your business site will draw customers to you directly.

- Have you researched how effective a press release can be for your business? If an editor of a newspaper, or a producer of a radio or television show likes your idea, they will do an interview about you and your product or service. This is free exposure that only costs you the price of a few letters and stamps.

- Look in the Yellow Pages under Television Stations, Radio Stations, Newspapers, and Magazines for the telephone numbers. Ask for the name of the Business Editor, or Producer. Send them a personalized, double-spaced press-release that is one to two pages in length. Follow up in two weeks to find out if they received your material. Don't ask them if they are going to do a story on you; simply remind them about your unique product, service, or idea.

- A newsletter is another inexpensive way for needed exposure. You could charge for a subscription, or send it out free each month, or every quarter, to existing, new, and prospective customers.

- T-shirts, pens, coffee mugs, paper weights, hats, etc., are a relatively inexpensive way to advertise your business. Check the costs by interviewing several 'Advertising Specialties' companies and include this in your business plan. These promotional items are a subtle reminder to your clients every time they see your name.

- Offer to give public speeches to several different organizations. The speaking and seminar business will enable you to develop new business relationships. Some organizations to choose from are:

  1. Business and Trade Organizations
  2. Civic Groups
  3. Convention Planners
  4. Service Organizers
  5. Business Firms and Organizations
  6. Political Affiliations
  7. Fraternal Organizations
  8. Athletic Clubs
  9. Professional Associations

As you scan the Yellow Pages, you will be pleasantly surprised at the number of organizations you probably never knew existed. Also, consider the various reference sources available in the library.

Clearly define the costs of promoting and holding your own seminar. Include costs for the room, beverages, overhead projectors, writing boards, tables, chairs, microphones, pens and paper, and your printed material.

Next, decide how much to charge for the seminar, or if it should be free. Take into consideration the cost of materials, audiovisuals, promotional costs, clerical support, transportation, lodging, etc.

Chapter Nine

Management Section

Your management team will be responsible for the success or failure of your business. As you develop your management team, keep this in mind: potential lenders and investment groups will only finance a company with a management team that has balance and the ability to provide the four essential elements of management:

1. Planning

2. Organization

3. Control

4. Leadership

Therefore, as you write this section of your plan, put down who will be in charge of certain responsibilities and tasks, and why they are qualified to manage this specific department or task within your company. Try to keep some kind of balance in your management team. As a whole, this team must have the personal, technical, and conceptual skills applicable to both the production of, and delivery of your product and/or service. Skills in marketing, finance, and operations are essential in creating an effective management team.

The strength of your management team must be strongly stated in your business plan. An organization with a formal structure is better able to raise capital and provide leadership and thus achieve its goals. When such structure is put in place first, your future goals are more easily accessible with less cost and waste of time.

Review data chart MT.1 on the next page and mentally review your proposed or existing management team. Use honesty in judging yourself and each member of the team. Do not let the "he is a nice guy" or "he never misses a day's work" syndrome sway truth from reality. Always choose the personnel that will drive your company to successful heights.

Complete data chart MT.1 (opposite page) for each key management team member.

Your Formal Organization

After completing data chart MT.1, begin to develop a formal organizational flow chart. Keep in mind the structure and size of your organization. It is reasonable for small to medium-sized businesses to have a management team consisting of one (or possibly two) key management personnel.

We strongly suggest that outside consultants and professionals be used to supply any missing expertise necessary to strengthen your management team. Example MT.1 provides a useful example of an overall organizational structure. Example MT.2 shows a further breakdown by department.

Incorporate Your Management Team Into Your Formal Organization

At this point, you have identified the abilities of your key management team and the formal organizational structure of your company. Now, in the final step, you must blend the two together to see if each key function within your organization can be met by at least one team member. Examples of major functions include:

- Marketing
- Sales
- Inventory control
- Operations
- Distribution
- Human resources

- Advertising
- Finance-Controller/Treasurer
- Purchasing
- Production
- Receiving
- Legal

Department of Manager _____

Name of Manager _____

Skills	**Grade**	**Grading Key**

Conceptual

Technical

Human

1 = Exceptional
2 = Good
3 = Average
4 = Shoud not be manager

Describe Strengths of Manager:

Describe Weaknesses of Manager:

Overall Grade (see key above)

Data Chart MT.1

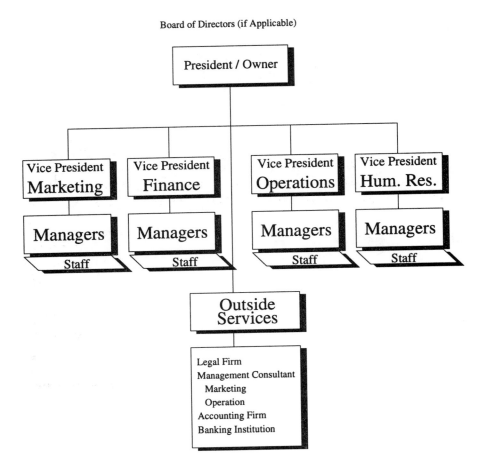

Board of Directors (if Applicable)

President / Owner

Vice President
Marketing

Vice President
Finance

Vice President
Operations

Vice President
Hum. Res.

Managers

Managers

Managers

Managers

Staff

Staff

Staff

Staff

Outside
Services

Legal Firm
Management Consultant
  Marketing
  Operation
Accounting Firm
Banking Institution

Example MT.1

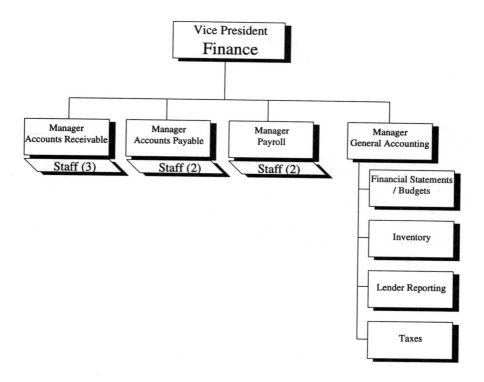

Use data chart MT.2 (on the next page) to incorporate key management personnel with key functions. For any responsibilities which cannot be covered by current management, check the column for outside services required. You may want to consider contacting outside consultants and professionals who specialize in these areas to assist you.

Now that you have determined your management structure and who should be a part of your management team, begin the documentation process.

Management

Tell why and by whom the company was started.

....

....

....

....

....

....

Management Team

There are several executives from the development staff who hold specific company positions:

1............................... , President

2............................... , Vice President

3............................... , Controller

4............................... , Marketing Manager

5............................... , Operations Manager

Explain combined experiences, strengths, leadership abilities and all positive characteristics.

Managers / Key Functions					Outside Services Needed

Data Chart MT.2

Responsibilities

List each manager separately and explain his/her various responsibilities. As you are listing responsibilities, try to determine if any are handling too much—or too little. Would some tasks be better delegated to or handled by other personnel? Be honest with yourself here. Remember, your honesty in these decisions will affect the bottom line of your company.

Outside Support

Include any outside professional consultant and industry expert who provides support for your management team.

1. Attorney: . . . .
2. Certified Public Accountant: . . . .
3. Business and Management Consultant: . . . .
4. Marketing Consultant: . . . .
5. Computer Consultant: . . . .
6. Temporary Agency: . . . .
7. Insurance Agent: . . . .

Management Résumés

Be sure to provide a brief, yet comprehensive résumé of the qualifications of each manager. Include references for key managers.

People/Talent Requirements

List current and future needs of required company staff. Estimate the number of employees as well as positions needed to effectively operate the business.

. . . .

. . . .

. . . .

. . . .

. . . .

. . . .

. . . .

Compensation

List salary histories, proposed salaries and other compensation for each management team member. Be sure to include bonuses, profit sharing plans, and other compensation arrangements.

. . . .

. . . .

. . . .

. . . .

. . . .

. . . .

. . . .

. . . .

If you currently have or plan to have a stock option plan, be sure to describe it.

. . . .

. . . .

. . . .

. . . .

Directors

Provide a complete list of directors. Be sure to include their name, professional credentials and any compensation you are providing.

. . . .

. . . .

. . . .

. . . .

. . . .

. . . .

. . . .

. . . .

. . . .

. . . .

Chapter Ten

Financial Projections

More Than Just Dollars and Cents

For most entrepreneurs, the development of an idea or concept is the easy part. Turning it into a profitable reality takes thorough research, especially as it relates to determining:

1. Potential markets

2. A realistic selling price for your products and services

3. Assets needed to produce and deliver

4. Costs associated to production

5. Advertising & promotion dollars needed to obtain market share

6. Fixed general & administration costs necessary to support the above, including the employee head count are necessary to support and operate your enterprise

In this section you should develop a set of financials that will include Profit and Loss Statements, Balance Sheets and Cash Flow Statements. A thorough understanding of how they are developed and conceived must be a top priority. Presenting potential lenders or investors with a set of financials is meaningless if they are incomprehensible to you. Therefore, before you dive in and begin crunching numbers, become familiar with the financial statements.

If uncertainty exists about your overall knowledge and understanding of financial statements, we suggest you do one or more of the following:

1. Purchase accounting learning and reference workbooks from a local bookstore.

2. Borrow reference accounting workbooks at your local library.

3. Take an accounting class at an accredited college or university.

4. Obtain help from an outside accounting firm familiar with your line of business.

Your Financial Management Tool

It is important for every business to prepare financial statements on a monthly basis, regardless of its size or structure.

Experience shows that many business owners/managers feel that monthly financial statements are either senseless or useless. THIS IS A BIG MIS-TAKE! Financial statements are KEY MANAGEMENT TOOLS. Take the time to learn and interpret what the financial statements are telling you. It could mean the difference between the success or failure of your business.

Determining Your #'s

By this stage of the game, whether you are a start-up or existing business, you should fully understand how to project, forecast, estimate, and calculate all items included in your financial statements.

If assistance is needed, we suggest you contact a competent accounting firm. They will be able to assist you in the completion of this portion of the business plan.

The pro forma schedules shown in the Sample Business Plan will aid you in your preparation. The Profit and Loss Statement, Balance Sheet, and Cash Flow Statement are already completed to help you understand how to produce these statements for your business plan.

For years one and two, we recommend presenting your Profit and Loss Statements on a monthly basis and your Balance Sheets and Cash Flow Statements on a quarterly basis. Present years three through five on an annual basis. Examples are presented in the Sample Business Plan.

Financial Projections

Here is the heart and soul of your business plan, the point in time where your vision is quantified in terms of dollars and cents and units of time (days, weeks, months, and years). Individuals interested in your plan will go through your financial projections with great care. Your financial projections should be broken down into monthly projections for years one and two, and annually thereafter, up to and including year five. If it is imperative to your business plan to include more than five years of financial projections, don't hesitate to do so. Based on this scenario, you should include the following financial statement projections: Profit and Loss Statement, Balance Sheet, and Cash Flow Statement.

Profit and Loss Statement—The marketing plan you have developed will be utilized in determining projected revenues over time. Typically, projections become outdated given the impact of all the variables at work in a given enterprise and its market environment. Adjustments will need to be made constantly as you implement mid-course corrections over time.

Next, calculate your cost of goods and/or services sold (COGS), as well as all your anticipated fixed overhead costs. Keep in mind that your COGS will generally fluctuate with revenue volume, while fixed overhead costs will exist on a continued basis.

The net difference of total revenues less total costs will determine the profit or loss of your enterprise.

Balance Sheet—The balance sheet gives a profile of the worth of your company's assets: cash, accounts receivable, inventory, machinery and equipment, land, etc.; *and*, all the company's liabilities: accounts payable, notes payable, taxes and interest payable, salaries and wages payable, etc.

The difference between the assets and the liabilities constitutes the net worth of the company (also called *owner's equity* or *stockholder's equity)*, at any particular moment in time. If you have a track record when the business plan is developed, as in an expansion of an existing operation, then the balance sheet may show considerable equity. If you are starting out with a new venture, the balance sheet may be very simple and show little or negative equity. Work with your local accounting team to develop the details of the balance sheet, if necessary.

Cash Flow Statement—The plotting of expected revenues, expenses, assets, liabilities and equity determines the level of cash flow. Cash flow totals are a critical index of how successful your business will be. Be sure to identify all changes in detail and leave nothing to the imagination. Be conservative, but realistic.

Please note, as in all number exercises, work with your accountant on the details.

Implementation Schedule

This portion of the business plan accomplishes the following:

- Identifies when you expect needed financing to kick in.

- Lists the main steps of the marketing campaign charted by date.

- Gives the scheduled dates of the production and delivery programs that will fulfill the obligations of sales.

The implementation schedule will enable you to coordinate and manage your enterprise in a systematic and controlled way. This section of your business plan is of critical importance both internally, as a management tool, and externally, as a means of persuading others that you have the "smarts" to put your project into effect.

Statement of Resource Needs

If you are using your business plan for the purpose of generating needed resources from lenders or investors, this document will summarize your precise needs (capital, terms, requirement date), and identify how the resources will be used.

In the case of financing, your cash-flow projections will, of course, reflect how these funds will be repaid.

In the case of capitalization involving equity partners, your projections will give an indication of the growth of equity and the anticipated timetable for the sharing of profits.

Sample: Statement of Resource Needs

Our objective, at this time, is to propel the company into a prominent market position. We feel that within five years HII will be in a suitable position for an initial public offering or profitable acquisition. To accomplish this goal, we have developed a comprehensive plan to intensify and accelerate our marketing activities, product development, services expansion, engineering, distribution, and customer service. To implement our plans, we require a line of credit of $150,000 for the following purposes:

1. Purchase one container of aluminum materials for inventory-$50,000.

2. Expand current operations into the rural areas of the United States-$30,000.

3. Procure production and computer equipment-$60,000.

4. Use as general working capital-$10,000.

Chapter Eleven

Executive Summary

As we have previously stated, the Executive Summary is that critical portion of an effective business plan, examined first by investors, yet completed after all other sections have been composed.

By preparing the Executive Summary last, you will be able to write it more easily and with greater impact, since you will have already compiled your data in other sections of your plan. Simply transfer the "sizzle" of the plan into concise paragraphs; these paragraphs become your Executive Summary.

Begin by explaining when your company was formed and what you sell, distribute, manufacture, etc.

Next, explain the purpose of your operation by stating what products/services you will provide your customers; then title this the "Statement of Purpose."

Indicate what phase of operation your business is presently in. Show projections which demonstrate that you will cut operating costs by a certain percentage and increase sales by a certain percentage. These two important items will result in a faster turn of cash flow to the company.

Next, refer to the section dealing with a "Mission Statement" and create your own statement.

Now give some background information on:

- The market

- Your customers' buying habits

- How you will educate your customers about your product/ service

- What type of quality products/services you sell

- Whether or not you will be able to buy from different suppliers at a lower cost

- Who you are buying your supplies from

- How much your operation has produced in annual sales over the past 3-5 years

- If you have operated at a loss, indicate why and then explain how you will correct this problem.

- Revenue projections for your next fiscal year, and projected annual growth rate (by percentage) for the next five years.

Now, begin explaining the Concept of your products and services. Use comparisons of similar products and services. Indicate any special training required for you or your staff, managers, and sales people, to properly manufacture, sell, and distribute your product/service.

Follow this up with whatever strategies you will use to meet the competition. Also, explain the market share you presently enjoy, or will enjoy.

The next step is to clarify your Target Market. Define your typical customer profile using the information that you wrote down earlier in Section Three. Also, indicate any additional products you believe your targeted market will respond to favorably.

Next, explain if your products are protected by copyright, trademark, and/or U.S. patent laws.

Are responses from customers or potential customers favorable? Indicate this also.

The next steps that you will take are relatively easy, since you have already compiled the data in other sections. Just give the most important details in a succinct fashion. The next "mini-sections" within your Executive Summary should be, in the following order:

- Objectives

- Management

- Marketing

- Finance

These sections, along with the previous sections, will compile a solid Executive Summary and give powerful, persuasive information to the reader.

Chapter Twelve

Appendix Section

Your Appendix should include all of the back-up documents to the data you have already shared.

In this section, you will want to provide as many supporting documents as you can. Two good places to find most of your important information will be the library and your customers.

Your public library carries previously written articles, publications, news-letters, reports and statistics that will help you verify your claims. Also look for Market Survey Data that has been collected by an independent surveying company.

Also in the Appendix, you should consider obtaining letters of reference. Your customers may be your strongest ally, when persuading potential investors with your project. If you can persuade loyal, satisfied customers, and/or respected people in the community to write you a letter of recommendation, you will be miles ahead of your competition. Get them to write the letter on their letterhead.

In the Appendix Section, also include your brochures, mechanical designs of your product, contracts, media information and surveys.

Appendix

In sum, this section of the business plan might include some or all of the following:

- Footnotes from the text (i.e., assumptions used in projections, further sources of information, etc.)

- Supporting documents

- Articles, clippings, and special reports

- Biographies

- Bibliographies

- Charts and graphs

- Copies of contracts and agreements

- Glossary of terms

- References: lenders, investors, or other bankers, suppliers etc., who can give positive feedback on your past performance.

Congratulations! You have compiled a good, solid business plan, if you have followed the steps in this book. Hopefully you have enjoyed the entire process. Chances are that if we had to bet wages on the outcome, you now understand your business much better.

Good luck in all your endeavors!

Chapter Thirteen

Practical Tips

Some general comments before you start:

Be Realistic

Build your business plan with a sense of realism and practicality. Do your homework carefully and think through every detail that could have a bearing on the success of your project. Your business plan should be a carefully crafted, practical document, geared towards performance, and not a speculative piece of fortune telling.

Document Your Claims

Where you base projections on specific assumptions (i.e., projections about market response to your goods and services), give evidence that these are based on facts. Assemble and apply expert opinion to substantiate your projections. Use sources such as newspaper and magazine articles, university studies, and interviews of prominent people familiar with your market.

Create a Unique Selling Advantage

If you have a "competitive edge," emphasize this advantage boldly. Make it your selling point and direct the consumer to associate his needs with your USA at the expense of the competitors.

Be Flexible

Your business plan, your "road map," allows you to check your position, velocity, and direction while keeping your objectives in mind. As you monitor your progress, you will periodically need to implement mid-course corrections. You will certainly need to adjust your business plan from time to time as your assumptions are updated according to real-life feedback from the "trenches," and as market conditions shift.

Use Technology to Good Advantage

Modern computers and computer software can be a tremendous help to you in developing portions of your business plan, especially the financial portions. With the help of computers, you can play "what if..." and gain valuable insight into future outcomes, based on strategic adjustment variables, such as pricing services in relation to variable costs. Have your local accounting experts explain the details, if necessary.

You might wish to invest in the equipment and software to service your own needs in these regards. Computer hardware is very much within reach of most budgets these days, and recent software developments place effective software programs within easy reach.

Attend to Packaging

The business plan should be clean, conservative, simple, well-prepared, clearly written, error-free, and appropriately bound. Your plan should look impressive, not slick. Let the visual form reflect the quality of the content. If you are presenting the business plan to prospective financial sources, you should bind the materials in such a way that they will open flat on a desk top. For "in-office" use, the business plan should be organized in a three-ringed binder, where updates can be easily incorporated.

Present the Business Plan Skillfully and Graphically

Consider using projection technology and similar support equipment when presenting your business plan to prospective funders. Presenting economic and chart-oriented information in attractive visual ways helps to solidify your position. Also, it speeds up presentations, makes the important facts quickly accessible, and reflects well on your ability as an effective business manager.

Chapter Fourteen

Sample Business Plan

Disclaimer

The information compiled in this Sample Business Plan was intended for use as an example only. All information in the Sample Business Plan is fictitious. Resemblance to any actual company is purely coincidental and is not intended to compete with, or to divulge proprietary ideas, company structure, or financial status of any company.

The information presented here is intended to be used as a guide only. We strongly recommend that the reader consult with an attorney, accountant, or other business advisor to verify that the format and structure is appropriate for his or her circumstances.

Home Improvements, Inc.

December 1992

Michael X. Swann

President

1234 East Main Street
Suite 1012
Anywhere, Arizona 85999
(602) 555-1919

Table of Contents

Executive Summary

In 1991, Home Improvements, Inc. (HII) was formed. During the past year, the company has positioned itself as a leader in the sales and distribution of durable and energy efficient aluminum siding and double pane windows.

The purpose of operation of the company is to provide customers with exterior aluminum siding that is attractive, yet provides a high degree of durability and energy efficiency to home owners and business owners.

Now, HII is at a point where it is entering two separate phases that are projected to cut operating costs by 15 percent and increase sales by 30 percent. By buying direct from the manufacturer, HII will realize better purchasing power and gain hands-on control of the manufacturing and assembly process. This will also cut down on delivery time to the customer, resulting in a faster cash flow to the company.

Our mission statement is as follows:

To provide customers with high-quality exterior aluminum siding and double pane windows where we can be proud of the integrity and craftsmanship of each product sold to the end-user, and offer superior customer service throughout the warranty phases of the product, always remembering that each customer may be a tremendous source of referral business to our company.

Background

For many years people have had one of two choices when considering purchasing exterior siding for their home or office:

1. Purchase high-quality aluminum siding at a premium price, or

2. Settle for a low-quality exterior siding made of wood composite, steel, or low-grade aluminum offered at a lower price.

Potential customers need to be educated on the important fact that all exterior siding is NOT made the same. When they settle for a lesser quality product, the end results are frustrating and costly.

At HII, we only sell the most highly-rated siding on the market today. The company will NOT sell cheaply manufactured products. However, to accomplish this, HII is currently forced to purchase materials from a single manufacturer. This presents a problem, because HII does not have an alternate source for the product; as well, it is costly to the customer and to HII in potential lost revenue due to higher prices.

As stated, HII is procuring its material as a complete product. Senior management has decided to buy raw material direct from other manufacturers. The product that HII purchases is manufactured in Asia and the United States. These companies have mastered the art of designing and manufacturing aluminum siding through advanced technology. Consequently, the product they provide is superior to any other on the market. Buying direct from the manufacturer will enable HII to save tens of thousands of dollars in the upcoming years, whereby the company can pass these savings on to the customer.

Our operation was producing $200,000 in sales by the end of 1991. This figure is represented by only eight months of operation. These results far exceed industry standards for a start-up enterprise of our size.

Revenue projected for fiscal year 1992, without external funding, is expected to be $480,000. Annual growth thereafter is projected to be an average of 15 percent per year through 1996.

Concept

The condition of the industry today is such that people are rapidly becoming aware of the need to protect their assets more than ever before. It has been shown that aluminum siding not only protects your home, but the beauty and attractiveness adds to its value.

Compared to competitive products, our product is made of the highest quality materials available. There are some companies that sell cheaply manufactured siding made of low-grade aluminum, steel, or wood composites.

The ability to educate customers on the superior quality of our product is a capability unique to our trained salespeople. Each of the company's sales personnel is required to complete a four-week training course before selling to the general public. This is absolutely essential to the success of our business, because of the "value-added" sale that salespeople will encounter. Since our product is made of higher quality materials, the cost of purchasing the material is higher. Plus, the company is presently buying a finished product direct from a single manufacturer. Once the "middleman" is eliminated, that will no longer be a problem.

Our strategy for meeting the competition is to buy raw material direct from various manufacturers and produce the finished product at HII. This will lower our prices to the customer. Presently, HII has a 30 percent market share in the Arizona market. Implementation of this strategy will result in a 20 percent increase in market share by the end of the first year.

Target Market

The typical customer profile for the company falls into two separate categories:

1. Households with an annual income of $30,000 to $50,000, and

2. Retired persons in medium- to upper-income housing.

HII is rapidly moving into its third marketing phase, namely expansion of its market base into rural geographical areas, and has relocated to a larger facility in Anywhere, Arizona.

One additional product that HII will provide its customers with is a state-of-the-art rain gutter system that is especially useful in draining water from the perimeter of a customer's house or property.

Another area that will eventually be developed includes:

An agreement with an Anywhere-based aluminum manufacturing company to supplement parts, thereby lowering shipping costs for some components of the aluminum siding. This will enable HII to purchase components from a local manufacturer.

All products from HII are protected by trademark and copyright laws, and patents from the original manufacturer.

Responses from customers indicate that our current product is enjoying an excellent reputation. Inquiries from prospective customers suggest that there is considerable demand for exterior aluminum siding and double pane windows. Relationships with leading OEMs (Original Equipment Manufacturers), retailers, major accounts, manufacturers, and distributors substantiate the fitness of the future outlook and potential of the industry.

Objectives

Our objective, at this time, is to propel the company into a prominent market position. We feel that within five years HII will be in a suitable condition for an initial public offering or profitable acquisition. To accomplish this goal, we have developed a comprehensive plan to intensify and accelerate our marketing activities, product development, services expansion, engineering, distribution, and customer service. To implement our plans we require a line of credit of $150,000 for the following purposes:

1. Purchase one container of aluminum materials for inventory-$50,000.

2. Expand current operations into the rural areas of the United States-$30,000.

3. Procurement of production and computer equipment-$60,000.

4. For general working capital-$10,000.

These items will enable HII to maximize sales with an extensive campaign to promote our products and services. It will also reinforce Customer Support services to handle the increased demands created by the influx of new orders and deepened penetration into new markets.

Management

Our management team is comprised of individuals whose backgrounds consist of 30 years of corporate development with major organizations, as well as over 25 years of sales and design within the home improvement industry.

Marketing

Conservative estimates suggest HII's market share, with our intensified and accelerated marketing plan, product development, manufacturing, and customer service, would be about thirty percent (30%) in the Arizona market.

The fundamental thrust of our marketing strategy consists of television, radio, printed advertising, and one-on-one selling in the home. Television and radio advertising have been the most successful marketing methods for HII, compared with flyers, direct mail, and display ads in magazines and newspapers.

We intend to reach prospective clients by continued advertising via television and radio. The marketing promotion tactics will consist of a New Leads Flow System. The customer calls the 1-800 number. The leads are forwarded to HII, whereby HII sends out product information. A subcontracted telemarketing firm calls the original leads and sets appointments for the sales personnel to go on.

None of the competitors of HII are advertising as intensely by television and radio. Our company can be characterized through our marketing efforts as the business that creates a positive and stable image for customers to see.

HII enjoys an established track-record of excellent support to our customers. Their expressions of satisfaction and encouragement are numerous, and we intend to continue our advances in the marketplace with more unique and instrumental offers.

Finance

In 24 months we will have reached our stated goals and objectives and our lending institution will be able to collect its return on investment. The original loan will be paid down to a balance of zero (as projected in the Balance Sheet for year three).

Present Situation

The current situation of the organization is very exciting. We have recently completed a move to a larger and more efficient facility. This move will enable the company to streamline its method of operation and increase its bottom line.

Market Environment:

The marketplace is undergoing tremendous technological change. New technology of exterior aluminum siding is making our product increasingly attractive, stronger, and less costly. We are poised now to take advantage of these changes, and expect to become an important supplier of aluminum siding and double pane windows.

Products and Services:

The present stage of exterior siding and double pane windows is the mature stage. This is primarily due to the strong influence of committed manufacturers and the demand for exterior siding.

Product Life Cycle:

Our current product line is primarily manufactured in the United States and Asia. Then it is assembled in Anywhere, Arizona. By buying direct from the manufacturer, HII will cut out 15 percent of our current costs. HII will then be able to pass these savings on to our customers.

Pricing and Profitability:

Current prices are increasing by 10 percent, due to rising labor and material costs in the U.S. and Asian marketplace.

Customers

Current customers are using our exterior siding and double pane windows for added home value, energy savings, storm protection, and noise reduction. They are requesting that we continue promoting our products in their area, so that the value of their neighborhoods will increase, especially during a tough real estate valuation period.

Distribution

We currently have one service center in Anywhere, Arizona. Our plans are to open additional offices and distribution centers in Indianapolis, Ind., and Knoxville, Tenn., once the results of operations warrant such centers. Once in place, these centers will reduce freight costs, as well as damage occurring during shipment.

Management:

Most of our management is in place, and HII enjoys a solid managerial staff with many years of experience directly related to the industry.

Financial Resources:

Current cash available is $22,500 (as of 12/31/91)

Our Current Ratio is:

$$\frac{\text{Current Assets}}{\text{Current Liabilities}}$$

$$\frac{51}{51} = 1{:}1\ (100\%)$$

Our Quick Ratio is:

$$\frac{\text{Cash + Accounts Receivable}}{\text{Current Liabilities}}$$

$$\frac{26}{51} = 0.51{:}1\ (51\%)$$

Objectives

The long term goal of Home Improvements, Inc. is to go public. With the additional capital provided, management intends to expand into rural America and purchase raw material, inventory, and equipment for the manufacturing and assembly of our products. With such an expansive network, we feel we can better serve our target market of middle- to upper-income households and retired persons.

Management also feels that with such a network, they will have stronger buying power and will be able to get more favorable pricing from manufacturers and vendors. This favorable pricing of material and equipment should allow the company to be more price competitive.

The final goal is to become a manufacturer of aluminum siding and maintain the company's distribution and sales operations.

Intermediate goals are to solidify our existing location and bring the company to a more profitable position. Long-term goals call for a 10 percent profit margin by the end of year five.

In order to achieve these goals, management has set two simple objectives for fiscal 1992. The primary objectives of our organization are:

1. To open up the rural sales offices upon funding.

2. To increase advertising spectrum through television and radio.

3. To purchase direct from OEMs.

4. To begin attending national and international trade shows.

5. To hire new personnel and purchase newer equipment.

6. To increase training for current and new salespeople.

For the company to achieve these immediate goals, the line of credit needs to be structured to long-term debt. This restructuring will better match the terms of the loan with the use of the proceeds. Long-term expansion and restructuring will also significantly improve the cash flow of the company over the next fiscal year.

The industry is expanding and more locations will be needed. Senior management expects to spend the majority of its time and marketing efforts on expanding current and new territories. The required funding is necessary to maintain expected growth. Net profits after tax from sales should approximate a total of $1.5 million over a ten-year period. Total sales for the same period of time are projected to be over $21 million.

Position for Growth Goals and Objectives

1. Understand customers, competition, and industry

2. Product/service/channel/customer congruency

3. Product/service life cycles

4. Growth by fields of interest

5. Balance people/management/business goals

6. Transition from single-point to distributed management

7. Operate at 50 employees

8. Develop values and culture

9. Hire the best people

We plan to maintain one distribution and service center in Anywhere, and add two sales and distribution offices and 20 sales-only offices by 1996.

Management

Home Improvements, Inc., was founded in 1991 by Michael X. Swann, who, after a careful study of the exterior siding industry, found a tremendous void of service and quality products.

This became the principal reason that Mr. Swann wanted to start his own distribution company in the industry. The opportunity to create an entity that offered superior service and products was reflected in his enthusiasm to begin Home Improvements, Inc.

The legal form of Home Improvements, Inc., is an Arizona Corporation.

Of the people who make up the development staff, there are several executives who hold the following positions:

> Michael X. Swann, President
>
> Mary V. Jonstone, Vice President Finance
>
> Roger Armstrong, Director of Marketing
>
> John Herbert, Manager of Production

The founders and key managers of HII have combined experiences exceeding 25 years in the siding and distribution industry.

The strength of the HII management team stems from the combined expertise in both management and sales areas. This has produced outstanding results over the past year.

The leadership and alignment characteristics of HII's management team have resulted in broad and flexible goal-setting to meet the ever-changing demands of the quick-moving marketplace that requires our products. This is evident when the team responds to situations requiring new and innovative capabilities.

Responsibilities

Michael X. Swann, President and General Manager

Manage market planning, advertising, public relations, sales promotion, merchandising and facilitating staff services. Identifying new markets, maintaining corporate scope and market research. Researching and identifying foreign markets.

Mary V. Jonstone, Vice President Finance

Management of working capital including: receivables, inventory, cash and marketable securities. Financial forecasting including: capital budget, cash budget, pro forma financial statements, external financing requirements and financial condition requirements.

Roger Armstrong, Director of Marketing

Manage field sales organization, territories, and quotas. Manage sales office activities, including customer/product support/service.

John Herbert, Manager of Production

Service, manufacturing, raw materials management, and installation.

Outside Support

An outside Board of Directors, including highly qualified business and industry experts, will assist our management team to make appropriate decisions and take the most effective action. However, they will not be responsible for management decisions.

Management Team

Michael X. Swann, President

Mr. Swann's professional experience includes many different areas in the sales and distribution arena. He has been involved in sales, marketing, and distribution of several services and products for large corporations, such as: Big Shoe Stores, Fresh Pine, Inc., and Home Siding 4 You. His experience covers many diverse areas and he has received several awards as the top sales representative for his efforts.

After learning the basic techniques of the siding industry, Mr. Swann worked with the development of sales and distribution for Home Siding 4 You (HSY).

While working for HSY, Mr. Swann was involved with the implementation of a sales and marketing program that increased the company's revenue by 45 percent.

There he enjoyed considerable success as National Sales Manager and Director of Sales and Marketing. However, he became interested in developing a more efficient way to operate a company within the same industry.

With ideas in mind, Mr. Swann conducted a feasibility study to determine the viability of a product capable of competing in the siding industry. When he found that such a market was worthwhile and could be developed, Mr. Swann formed Home Improvements, Inc., in 1990.

Mary V. Jonstone, Vice President Finance

Ms. Jonstone comes from a diverse background in finance and management. She served as a Department Manager for 12 years at VALUE Department Stores and House and Yard, Inc.

Ms. Jonstone has been overseeing the Finance Department for Home Improvements, Inc., since the company's inception.

Roger Armstrong, Director of Marketing

Mr. Armstrong's background in sales and marketing has been a big asset to the company. After earning a degree in marketing, Mr. Armstrong went to work as a sales representative for Steel Boxes, Inc. He enjoyed a successful career there.

Mr. Armstrong then moved on to a management position with the multinational corporation Better Products, Inc. As a manager, he was involved with day-to-day operations of inventory control, hiring and training personnel, and developing departmental policies and procedures.

Mr. Armstrong also worked for Top Aluminum for three years, where he earned the Top Sales Representative Award for the entire United States.

Mr. Armstrong has enjoyed a high degree of success at HII. He has helped develop the present sales and marketing structure of the company. As a sales professional, he trains and assists new sales representatives. As a Marketing Manager, he is involved with development of marketing strategies and market research.

John Herbert, Manager of Production

Mr. Herbert has a solid ten years of qualified experience specifically in the siding industry. His knowledge of the requirements for proper installation is an important asset to the company.

Mr. Herbert is responsible for several areas related to each project. He oversees everything from the bidding process to the completion of the job, which also includes the timely satisfaction of the customer.

People/Talent We Require:

The HII development team recognizes that additional staff is required to properly support marketing, sales, and research, as well as functions.

Currently, HII is composed of eight personnel. Over the next five years, 50 personnel will be required to meet the demands of the projected market. These staff requirements will include personnel in the following areas:

    Management
    Marketing
    Sales
    Engineering
    Customer Relations
    Administration
    Manufacturing
    Skilled Assembly Labor
    Field Service Technicians

Product Description

HII products are manufactured in Japan, Korea, Florida, and South Carolina, then assembled in Anywhere, Arizona. State-of-the-art tooling and strict quality control procedures produce dependable, custom-hardened, aluminum alloy siding.

To fight against weather conditions, each panel is technologically slotted and overlaid on fiberglass insulation of high density. This provides extra insulation value inside the HII siding panel during the entire year.

Trim pieces and eave underpanels are made from extruded aluminum that give the final touches to an attractive product along with securing additional energy efficiency.

The colors available are:

> White
>
> Cream
>
> Dark Brown
>
> Dark Wood Grain
>
> Beige
>
> Sky Blue
>
> Aqua Green
>
> Sunflower Yellow

Custom colors can be chosen from HII's Custom chart, which includes an additional forty colors to choose from. Delivery times for custom colors are usually three weeks longer than for our standard colors.

Pay Back

For most customers, HII siding and double-pane windows will pay for themselves in terms of energy savings within 12 years. Research has proved that between 10 percent and 15 percent savings of annual energy costs may be realized by each homeowner. During the hotter months, HII siding and windows intercept solar radiation, thus providing insulation value that allows air conditioners to work about 30 percent less.

In the winter, HII aluminum siding and double-pane windows provide a pleasant insulating blanket. This insulated exterior shield keeps the cold air from entering, and keeps the heat inside the home.

Here are a few of the other outstanding features of HII aluminum siding:

- Premium quality and efficiency

- Lower warranty costs

- Improved energy-efficiency

- Improved home value

Even a moment's reflection will prove that personal satisfaction in one's home is worth a fortune. There really isn't a price one could place on the peace of mind that our products give to the home owners. These are some of the nonmonetary benefits of owning HII aluminum siding.

Useful Purpose and Key Benefits

These combined capabilities provide added value, energy savings, noise abatement, and protection from storms.

This, in turn, can be used to create a sense of greater need in the minds of customers. These are benefits that are worth the extra money and, during our history, have convinced customers to buy from HII.

Tests

Completed tests have shown that HII aluminum siding has been subjected to many tests of impact by hard and soft objects. These tests are in accordance with the common rules of the Product Durability Testing Requirements set forth by U.S. regulations. The test resulted in a performance that is highly superior to that which the regulations require.

Product/Service Life Cycle

The life cycle of HII aluminum siding is estimated to be 60 years. The manufacturer's warranty covers all exterior parts for 5 years.

Market Analysis

Market Definition

Currently, the Arizona market distribution is shared by nine participants. Home Improvement, Inc., enjoys approximately 30 percent of this market share. There are four other major competitors that share an approximate 60 percent, and the remaining competitors share a combined total of 10 percent.

The stability of this market segment is expected to increase. However, some volatility has been introduced to the market with the announcement of a national recession.

The exterior aluminum siding market is growing at a rapid rate: The market for siding in the United States is virtually untapped. The United States is a very immature market with tremendous growth potential.*

Over the past 3 years, companies have developed and shown the additional features that can be provided for this type of industry. These companies have focused on the use of technological advances to steadily improve the quality of aluminum in exterior siding.

The report, New Consumer Product Reports, also states that firms selling home value-added products will prosper greatly in the coming decade.

Strengths

In marketing, our most powerful assets are the uses of television and radio for advertising and promotion. The public awareness of the HII products and services has been greatly enhanced due to our intense advertising policies.

With a 30 percent market share, HII has the largest share of the market spread among six other competitors. This is not only due to our marketing strategies, but includes our superior customer service.

Weaknesses

There are some handicaps inherent in our market. The only notable marketplace disadvantages are the prices that customers believe they will have to pay for their home beauty and energy-efficiency. Typically, an average job will cost around $13,000, if the entire home is covered with siding and double-pane windows.

Corporate weaknesses, at this time, consist only of not enough sales personnel. However, we are taking steps to interview competent sales professionals, which we feel should alleviate this problem.

*Source: Westeck, Improved Contracting Unit

There are no environmental threats with our product.

Customers

The person who influences the decision to buy is the housewife. She will also permit the purchase to be made. Generally speaking, the housewife is the person who will also choose the color and the areas where the siding will be added to the home.

The most typical customers for our product/service are households earning between $30,000 and $50,000 per year, and retired persons living in middle- to upper-class housing developments.

It is likely that potential customers are going to be familiar with aluminum siding and double-pane windows and that they will readily accept our advertising approach, provided that we educate them in the proper manner. It is also important to point out that our marketing and advertising efforts have been targeted to people concerned about adding value and energy efficiency to their homes, and to retired individuals.

It is easy to understand why the principal buying motives are geared toward our products: because retired persons and housewives are looking for added comfort in and around their homes.

Research indicates that these groups of customers are not as sensitive to pricing differences among competitors. In fact, research also indicates that these people are willing to spend their money on ways that will improve their way of life. It is our task to educate the customer on the superior quality of our products and service.

Housewife

     Age: 35-65

     Income: . . . . Fixed

     Sex: . . . . Female

     Family: . . . . Full nest

     Geographic: . . . . Suburban

     Occupation: . . . . Housewife

     Attitude: . . . . Security-minded

Married Couples

     Age: 35-55

     Income: . . . . Medium to high

```
Sex: ...................................... Male or female

Family: ........................ Married or no children

Geographic: ................................. Suburban

Occupation: ..................................... Varies

Attitude: ........... Security-minded, energy-conscious
```

Older Couple

```
Age: ........................................... 55-75

Income: ............................... High or fixed

Sex: .................................... Male or female

Family: ................................... Empty nest

Geographic: ................................. Suburban

Occupation: ..................... White-collar or retired

Attitude: ............................. Security-minded
```

Elderly

```
Age: ............................................. 70+

Income: .................................... Fixed

Sex: ................................... Male or Female

Family: ................................... Empty nest

Geographic: ................................. Suburban

Occupation: ................................. Retired

Attitude: ............................ Security-minded
```

Competition

Competitive threats today come primarily from three major competitors and three other dealers in Arizona.

HII's products perform in virtually all situations where there is a home or office where the siding and windows can be added.

The ability to offer superior beauty, along with full capability to provide an insulating blanket for the home or office, is unique for such an attractive addition to any building or structure.

Our research indicates that the performance of HII's products is superior to anything else on the market today. In all comparisons, the products that HII provides have more features, as well as superior performance, than competitive products. In most cases, the number of differences is substantial. A complete technical comparison is available.

Competitive Products and Services:

Companies that compete in the U.S. market are: Home Siding 4 You (HSY), U.S. Aluminum (USA), North East Siding (NES), and Quality Home Products (QHP). All companies mentioned charge competitive prices.

Most of these products do not provide the same capabilities when the construction of the siding is compared to HII's product.

For example, our aluminum siding has been subjected to many trials of impact with hard and soft objects, in accordance with the common rules of the Product Durability Testing Requirements as set forth by U.S. regulations. It turned out to be highly superior to what the regulations require.

Competitive Roundup:

The following chart illustrates how HII compares with the competition in several different key areas.

	Competition	HII
Estimated Share of Market (HSY, USA, NES, QHP)	60%	30%
Rank:1=Weak to 5=Strong		
Product line	4	5
Quality	4	5
Technology	4	5
Advertising effectiveness	2	5
Sales force excellence	3	5
Distribution	3	4
Seriousness of competition	3	5
Price	4	4
Installation	4	5
Ease of use	4	5
Appearance	3	5
Quality	3	5
Design	4	5
Useful life	4	4
Responsiveness	3	5
24-Hour availability/support	1	5
Technical expertise	4	5
Repair service	3	5
Efficiency	3	5
Guarantee/warranty	5	5
On-time capability	4	5
Upgrades	4	4
Standing in industry	3	5

Observations and Conclusions:

It appears from the above information that some of our competition is faring well in this tough market. However, it is clearly apparent that HII is offering a superior product and service at a competitive price.

Marketing Strategy

HII's marketing strategy is to enhance, promote, and support the fact that our products/services are superior to others in the market.

Comprehensive Plan

The overall marketing plan for our product is based on the following fundamentals:

1. The segment of the market(s) planned to reach.

2. Distribution channels to be used in order to reach market segment: television, radio, sales representatives and mail order.

3. Share of the market expected to capture over a fixed period of time.

To prove the value of exterior aluminum siding and double-pane windows, we will demonstrate two areas that sell our products: Added Value and Energy Efficiency. These two areas are a great concern to the customers who purchase our products.

The lack of exterior aluminum siding and double-pane windows in everyday situations is demonstrated by the numerous studies on neighborhood values and energy-efficiency.

Because our product is constructed with a high-grade aluminum and installed over superior insulation, an extra value is added to the home year round. Based on an actual comparison, our product saves an average of 10 percent to 15 percent in energy costs.*

Product Strategy

Exterior aluminum siding and double-pane windows should be treated as a long-term product. The consumer can recoup his investment within the term of a 30-year mortgage, if one only considers energy savings. However, if one considers the added value of property, the amount of return on return on investment is immeasurable.

Positioning

Our products are seen by consumers as a product that protects their homes, as well as protecting their pocketbooks, through energy savings.

Its unique advantages can be exploited to arrive at a winning position in the consumer's mind.

In terms of market segmentation advantages, we can use these factors already mentioned to arrive at a winning position here.

* Source: County Gas & Electric

By repositioning our product from a cost to an investment in the home, and as an overall attractively appealing package, exterior aluminum siding and double-pane windows become a smart investment for any consumer.

Outside Suppliers

HII is presently using the firm Superior Media Marketing for the overall television and radio marketing strategy. This has been a good relationship that has lasted since the inception of the company. Superior Media Marketing has the buying power, technical, and marketing expertise that is necessary for a successful campaign. HII is also working closely with TRICO Business Solutions for additional marketing consulting.

Marketing Responsibilities

The President of HII, Mr. Swann, will be responsible for these marketing decisions:

> New business development
>
> Dealer and OEM support
>
> Sales generation tools
>
> Corporate graphics standard
>
> Brandmark recognition
>
> Direct response promotion
>
> Telemarketing scripts/training
>
> Product position and identification
>
> Selling tactics (Refer to section on Selling Tactics for details.)
>
> Advertising and promotion (Refer to section on Advertising and Promotion for details.)

Includes:

> Company positioning (identity) within market:
>
>> The identity is consistent throughout all areas of communication
>
> Promotional tools:
>
>> Brochures and catalogs
>>
>> Other collateral materials

Advertising:

    Targeted advertisements

    Media selection and strategy

Sales support:

    Distributor and retailer support packages

    Representative support (sales tools)

    Communication within channels of distribution

Feedback loops:

    Lead generation

    Lead referral and follow-up systems

    Information gathering and dissemination

Strategy Review

Based on the marketing strategies, advertising and promotion, and selling tactics sections, the following questions have been reviewed and answered:

Do the strategies define means for achieving the objectives management sets?

Are the strategies consistent with our evaluation of the marketplace and our capabilities?

Is the return on investment sufficient to justify the risks?

What are the chances of a competitor executing a similar strategy? In that case, what would happen?

Have we made sure our strategies are based on facts, and not assumptions?

Does the overall strategy leave us critically vulnerable to a shift in market behavior?

Is our appraisal of the competition open-minded and honest?

Is our strategy legal?

Is the success of our strategy based on our ability window? What are the chances of failure?

Have we thoroughly examined alternative strategies? Do we have a sound, deductive rationale for our recommendations?

Advertising and Promotion

Home Improvements, Inc. (HII), recognizes that the key to success at this time requires extensive promotion. This must be done aggressively and on a wide scale. To accomplish sales goals, HII will require an extremely capable advertising agency and public relations firm.

The company plans to do most of its advertising on television and radio, in major metropolitan cities.

Once an agency selection is made, its assistance in developing a comprehensive advertising and promotion plan will be needed. Advertising will be done independently and cooperatively with Distributors, OEMs, retailers, and companies with whom HII has joint marketing/sales relationships.

Advertising and Promotion Objectives

The primary reason for such a heavy advertising campaign is to position HII as the leading supplier of exterior aluminum siding and double-pane windows in the U.S. market.

By so doing, HII plans to generate qualified sales leads for field sales representatives, who will be able to take faster action in closing sales. This will be accomplished by cutting out 80 percent of their time directly involved with prospecting. HII's experience has been that sales representatives can optimize the impact of their time by using a promotional campaign like the one that will be used to generate leads.

Media Objectives

The objectives that HII will obtain with a television and radio advertising campaign will give the company greater public awareness. Television and radio advertising will establish an image of HII as a solid organization that is very professional, completely reliable, and highly visible in the market. This is in addition to the fact that HII has maximized efficiency in selection and scheduling of sales representatives' time.

Media Strategy

It is the aim of senior management to position HII in select primary publications, radio stations and television stations with highly specific market penetration. Therefore, it is important to schedule adequate frequency to impact the market with a positive corporate image and superior products and services.

Plans are to work closely with a reputable advertising agency to maximize ad life with monthly and weekly exposure of the advertisements.

To get the most out of our promotional budget, the media coverage will focus on two targeted audiences:

110

1. Households concerned about home value and energy-efficiency, and

2. Retired individuals in high income areas.

An advertising campaign will be built around the added value and energy-efficiency of our product, beginning with a "who we are" position and supporting it with ads that reinforce the added value and energy-efficiency message. It is important that a consistent message and frequency be maintained throughout the year.

Advertising Campaign

The best way to reach our potential customers is to develop an intense advertising campaign promoting the company's basic premise—"Value you can count on!"

To maintain our stable image, the delivery and tone of promotional statements will be based on hard-driving reality that creates a sense of urgency to protect one's assets and energy savings.

Ads will convey the look and feel of a home that is attractive, comfortable and energy-efficient.

Research indicates that television and radio advertising is not heavily used by any of our competitors. The consumer mindset is that they are eager to purchase a product that will offer a solution to possibly diminishing property values that their neighborhoods may be facing.

Ideally, after becoming familiar with our product and service(s), consumers will be able to take action by calling a toll-free number to place their order, or request that additional information be sent to them, or set up an appointment with a sales representative.

To eliminate the biggest objections to immediate action, the advertisements must address known and anticipated objections, such as how much is their property worth?

Because HII's product is so unique, it is important to develop a promotional campaign that is consistent and easy to understand.

Accordingly, HII has created a system of research and response to ensure the maximum benefit of its advertising dollars. One way to measure the effectiveness of its advertising is to count the number of responses and purchases per 100 customers given a particular ad.

Research shows that television commercials will bring in an average of 48 leads per day. Further research indicates that for every 100 phone-in leads, the following results are typical:

29% Are not really interested at this time

18% Do not own their home, or are not interested in buying aluminum siding for their future home

3 % Give incorrect information (i.e., wrong phone number)

10% Request that we call at a later date

40% Turn into an actual appointment

From the 40 percent, research indicates that approximately 20 percent, or one in every five appointments, turns into a sale.*

Preliminary Media Schedule

	Customers	Budget
Projected sales (per month)	15	$105,000
Monthly cost of advertising		25,000
Anticipated Profits (per month)		8,000

We expect to reach a total monthly audience of 10 million potential customers.

Promotion

In addition to standard advertising practices, HII will gain considerable recognition through these additional promotional mediums:

- Trade programs that are offered throughout the Southwest and Northwest Regions.
- Press releases sent to major radio stations, newspapers, and magazines.
- Radio advertising on secondary stations.

The number of trade shows attended will be increased from two to five each year. These shows will be attended both independently and with companies with which HII has joint marketing/sales or OEM agreements.

Reports and papers will be published for trade journals and technical conferences. These reports will be written by an outside consulting agency and edited by senior management.

Incentives

As an extra incentive for customers to remember HII's name and the service that HII provides, plans are to distribute coffee mugs, hats, and tee shirts with the company logo and slogan. This will be a gratis service that will be provided to keep the name in front of customers.

*Source: Marketing Survey Source, Inc.

Direct Mail

In the past, the company has used direct mail as a marketing avenue to generate leads. The type of direct response piece was a house-to-house coupon mailer. This campaign did not generate the responses hoped for.

Senior management was presented with ideas of new plans to refocus direct mail efforts in the form of personal letters, with a detachable return voucher. Research has proved that this is a more effective way of reaching our targeted markets, with a greater success ratio.

Corporate Capabilities Brochure

Objective: To portray HII as the leading supplier of state-of-the-art exterior aluminum siding.

Recommended contents: Use the current corporate brochure with minor revisions to the first page, displaying new management, sales personnel and our new facilities.

Management: With the new brochure, a portrayal of dedicated experienced, and professional managers is important in order to depict a team that will ensure complete satisfaction.

Sales: Portray HII's full selling team, including representatives and distributors, as a savvy, dedicated support group with one overriding mission: customer satisfaction.

Marketing: Present the marketing department in its role of market research, product development, new product management, etc., providing improved product ideas to the user.

Sales Support Collateral Materials

An additional form of advertising in the home will be used by each sales representative. Each will carry a Video Introduction Tape and give a home presentation. The video tape will be designed to give an accurate description of all the benefits of having exterior aluminum siding. It will enable sales representatives to close more sales, as well as attract new distributors.

In addition, each sales representative will carry a presentation binder that is organized in a "flip chart" format to keep their thoughts in a unified and easy to understand style.

The following is a list of items that will assist sales representatives with the communications process during their sales presentations:

- Ads
- Brochures
- Business Cards
- Catalogs
- Charts
- Data Sheets
- Direct Mail
- Resumes
- Handouts
- Videos
- Newsletters
- Post Cards
- Price Lists
- Promotions
- Proposals
- Questionnaires
- Reports
- Stationery
- Telephone Scripts
- Letters

Investment in Advertising and Promotion

For the first 12 months of the project, advertising and promotion will require $48,000. On a regular basis, HII feels that it can budget its advertising investment at 15 percent of total sales.

This figure is necessary because of the specific goals HII plans to meet. Industry averages for dollars spent on advertising and promotion are considerably less, because competitors are not using television and radio as a marketing tool.

Selling Tactics

Current Selling Methods

HII's marketing strategy incorporates plans to sell its line of products/services through several channels:

Executive selling

Direct sales force

Distributors

Mail-order/direct response

Telemarketing

Joint marketing relationships

Executive Sales

Because our customers tend to be overly conscientious about spending large amounts of money, it is important that our company president and senior managers present our product and service to our customers on occasion.

Direct Sales

The majority of sales will be through direct sales by the HII sales staff. HII anticipates hiring ten additional sales representatives to cover additional territories and markets to sell specific products.

We have chosen to use a direct sales force because our products require considerable customer education and postsales support directly from the company. Our price point, pricing structure, and profits are such that our cost of sales warrants that sales be handled on an individual basis in this manner.

Distributors

One of the key elements designed into the HII marketing plan is the targeting of its distributors. It is important to select distribution channels already in existence and staffed with professionals possessing appropriate backgrounds and clientele.

HII products are pertinent to the nature of the distributor's business and to the well-being of its customer base. Also, it is significantly less difficult for us to reach distributors and educate them as to the benefits available in using exterior aluminum siding.

This strategic marketing approach takes full advantage of the tremendous momentum inherent in the fact that these professionals are already involved with parallel products and services. They already have expertise and have been practicing in their field for a long time.

By operating within these distribution channels in this manner, we feel that we can maintain control of our market. In addition, we can generate growth at a reasonable pace and obtain excellent sales results.

- See Distribution Section for detailed plan of action.
- See also Advertising and Promotion section on "Direct Mail," regarding appropriate distributors.

Distribution

HII will use several different distribution channels. The determining factors in choosing these channels are:

- Customer profile
- Geography
- Seasonal concerns
- Efficient use of funds
- Feasibility of using channels of similar products already on the market

Method

The primary means of distribution will be through company sales representatives. Secondary means of distribution will be through third-party distributors.

An important advantage of these alternate channels is flexibility. By using more than one method, HII will have more control and also more options with which to respond to special needs and circumstances.

Other features of our secondary channels are low cost, quick start-up, increased capacity to reach more customers that are not necessarily influenced by advertising and promotional methods.

Coverage

Metropolitan target areas indicate the highest level of consumer interest.

Because our distribution network is easy and cost-efficient to implement, we can enjoy delivery almost immediately. This, in turn, will reduce shipping time and increase customer satisfaction. To date, none of our competitors is able to achieve this.

Roll-Out Program

We have selected from ten key market areas based on proximity—easy to sell into, contact, deliver to, have customers come to, etc.

Trade Incentives

It is the intention of senior management to offer incentives to regional distributors, such as allowances, co-op accruals, warehouse flushing promotions, etc.

Customer Service

Our customers emphasize that support is one of their major concerns. They are constantly impressed with the support provided by HII. Hot-line service is currently available to all customers enrolled in a maintenance/support program.

We intend to provide free post-sale consultation for customers. The purpose for this service is to ensure customer satisfaction and loyalty and, in addition, allow us to increase sales as well as maintain a high profile within our service area.

Another service to add value is to provide warehousing of customer inventory. This allows us to book larger orders and provide faster order response.

Support to distributors is provided as required. This allows them to perform efficiently as a sales force. We intend to treat the distributors as an extension of the HII direct sales force and they will be given the same support as the HII internal sales staff.

Technical support to marketing and sales functions will be strengthened. Pre- and post-sales situations involving the application, presentation, and demonstration of HII products will be supported by our customer service and marketing staff.

Returns and Cancellation Policy

At this time, general trade customs for handling cancellations are to provide a full refund of any down payment, if a cancellation occurs within 3 business days from the signing of the contract.

Refunds are made only on the price of the package, plus applicable taxes, and do not include shipping costs.

Credit card refunds are credited to the customer's account and cash or check payments are refunded within 30 days of receipt of returned merchandise in good condition.

Business Relationships

HII has formed some very important relationships with major companies in the industry. The following is a list of existing relationships:

OEM Relationships

OEMs (Original Equipment Manufacturers)—The major advantage of selling through OEMs is to provide a means of more rapidly penetrating the market. Also, these relationships provide HII with national coverage through established sales forces.

We are presently buying from, or developing relationships with, the following OEMs:

1. Craft Aluminum, Inc.

2. All Seal Windows

3. Custom Improvements, Inc.

4. Quality Built Materials

5. Protection Plus, Ltd.

Joint Marketing Agreements

Joint marketing with established companies will produce revenues, credibility, and market presence.

HII is pursuing joint marketing agreements with other organizations to further the name of our products and services in the U.S. markets. Our plans include having them market our exterior aluminum siding and double-pane windows within their product line.

Third-Party Supplier Agreements

We feel that we require additional components to enhance the attractiveness of our products and services to customers. Because we do not currently have the resources to procure the exterior aluminum siding from OEMs, we rely on a single manufacturer for the availability of our product line.

Financial Projections

Current Assets

1. Cash—reflects limited amount of cash on hand at any balance sheet date. Positive generation of cash is to be applied against outstanding loan.

   Cash on hand can be eliminated upon implementation of a "direct disbursement" program for both checking and payroll accounts. This will allow Home Improvements, Inc. to maximize the management of cash by borrowing only when required to, and to apply monies received directly against the bank loan payable.

2. Accounts Receivable—are minimal to Home Improvements, Inc. Company policy dictates cash before installation or approved financing from reputable finance companies on the majority of projects.

3. Inventory—is to be purchased on a container-load basis at a precalculated reorder point determined by lead times provided by the manufacturers. Product on hand will be items already categorized as "work-in-process." Stock available for sale is scheduled to turn over in a 6- to 8-week period.

Fixed Assets

1. Production and assembly of the aluminum siding requires light machinery. The major piece of equipment required is a 20-inch radial-arm saw for aluminum cutting. This equipment will be purchased on an as-needed basis with available cash funds.

2. Thirty thousand dollars has been scheduled for 1st quarter 1993 for the purchase of new commercials, new equipment and office furniture.

3. Depreciation—Equipment and furniture have been considered to be either 7-year or 5-year property per Modified Accelerated Cost Recovery System (MACRS). Whole year depreciation has been estimated for all equipment.

Liabilities

1. Accounts Payable—Includes amounts due on inventory purchases as well as non-inventory items such as supplies, tools, telephone, travel and entertainment.

2. Taxes Payable—for unpaid Federal, State, FICA, FUTA, SUI, and medical withholding based on current and expected headcount.

Selling, General, and Administration

1. Officer Wages—for all years have been reflected at market value.

2. Employee Wages—includes all Home Improvements, Inc. employees including sales, general administration and warehouse. Wage increases for non-officer employees are calculated at 5 percent per annum.

3. General Administration Expenses—have been increased annually by approximately 6 percent to reflect inflationary increases.

Break-Even Analysis:

Projected for the first quarter of 1992   ($ 000)

Sales			34
COGS	Materials	7	
	Labor	4	
Total COGS			11
Gross profit margin			23
Selling expenses	Commissions	3	
	Advertising	4	
Total selling expenses			7
Profit before G&A expenses			16
Total G&A expenses			16
Break-even			0

Appendix

Letters of Recommendation

Market Survey Data

Television and Radio Advertising Statement

Property Value and Statistics

Mechanical Designs of the Product

Company Brochures

Note:

The appendix should include all documentation that will support and add value to your organization. The above outline only covers several examples of items that could be included in the appendix of your business plan.

HOME IMPROVEMENTS, INC.
PROFIT & LOSS STATEMENT
YEAR ONE - 1992
Rounded to Hundreds ($00)

	1	2	3	4	5	6	7	8	9	10	11	12	YEAR ONE
SALES	30,0	30,0	30,0	40,0	40,0	40,0	40,0	40,0	40,0	50,0	50,0	50,0	480,0
COGS—MATERIALS	6,0	6,0	6,0	8,0	8,0	8,0	8,0	8,0	8,0	10,0	10,0	10,0	96,0
LABOR	3,6	3,6	3,6	4,8	4,8	4,8	4,8	4,8	4,8	6,0	6,0	6,0	57,6
TOTAL COGS	9,6	9,6	9,6	12,8	12,8	12,8	12,8	12,8	12,8	16,0	16,0	16,0	153,6
GROSS PROFIT/MARGIN	20,4	20,4	20,4	27,2	27,2	27,2	27,2	27,2	27,2	34,0	34,0	34,0	326,4
SELLING—COMMISSIONS	3,0	3,0	3,0	4,0	4,0	4,0	4,0	4,0	4,0	5,0	5,0	5,0	48,0
ADVERTISING	3,6	3,6	3,6	4,8	4,8	4,8	4,8	4,8	4,8	6,0	6,0	6,0	57,6
TOTAL SELLING	6,6	6,6	6,6	8,8	8,8	8,8	8,8	8,8	8,8	11,0	11,0	11,0	105,6
PROFIT BEFORE G&A	13,8	13,8	13,8	18,4	18,4	18,4	18,4	18,4	18,4	23,0	23,0	23,0	220,8
TOTAL G&A (SCHEDULE)	15,7	15,7	15,7	15,8	15,8	15,8	16,1	16,1	16,1	16,2	16,2	16,2	191,4
PROFIT(LOSS)BEFORE TAX-	-1,9	-1,9	-1,9	2,6	2,6	2,6	2,3	2,3	2,3	6,8	6,8	6,8	29,4
ESTIMATED INCOME TAX													7,4
PROFIT AFTER TAX													22,0

HOME IMPROVEMENTS, INC.
GENERAL & ADMINISTRATIVE EXPENSE
YEAR ONE - 1992
Rounded to Hundreds ($00)

	1	2	3	4	5	6	7	8	9	10	11	12	YEAR ONE
SALARIES—EMPLOYEES	8,8	8,8	8,8	8,8	8,8	8,8	8,8	8,8	8,8	8,8	8,8	8,8	105,6
SALARIES—OFFICERS	2,0	2,0	2,0	2,0	2,0	2,0	2,0	2,0	2,0	2,0	2,0	2,0	24,0
PAYROLL TAXES/BENEFITS	1,0	1,0	1,0	1,0	1,0	1,0	1,0	1,0	1,0	1,0	1,0	12,0	
VEHICLE EXPENSE	,3	,3	,3	,3	,3	,3	,3	,3	,3	,3	,3	,3	3,6
INSURANCE	,2	,2	,2	,2	,2	,2	,2	,2	,2	,2	,2	,2	2,4
LEGAL & ACCOUNTING	,2	,2	,2	,2	,2	,2	,2	,2	,2	,2	,2	,2	2,4
GENERAL OFFICE EXP	,1	,1	,1	,1	,1	,1	,2	,2	,2	,2	,2	,2	1,8
POSTAGE	,1	,1	,1	,1	,1	,1	,2	,2	,2	,2	,2	,2	1,8
OFFICE SUPPLIES	,2	,2	,2	,2	,2	,2	,3	,3	,3	,3	,3	,3	3,0
TELEPHONE	,5	,5	,5	,6	,6	,6	,6	,6	,6	,7	,7	,7	7,2
RENT	,8	,8	,8	,8	,8	,8	,8	,8	,8	,8	,8	,8	9,6
UTILITIES	,2	,2	,2	,2	,2	,2	,2	,2	,2	,2	,2	,2	2,4
DEPRECIATION	,9	,9	,9	,9	,9	,9	,9	,9	,9	,9	,9	,9	10,8
TRAVEL	,2	,2	,2	,2	,2	,2	,2	,2	,2	,2	,2	,2	2,4
ENTERTAINMENT	,1	,1	,1	,1	,1	,1	,1	,1	,1	,1	,1	,1	1,2
MISCELLANEOUS	,1	,1	,1	,1	,1	,1	,1	,1	,1	,1	,1	,1	1,2
TOTAL G&A EXPENSE	15,7	15,7	15,7	15,8	15,8	15,8	16,1	16,1	16,1	16,2	16,2	16,2	191,4

HOME IMPROVEMENTS, INC.
QUARTERLY BALANCE SHEET
YEAR ONE - 1992
Rounded to Hundreds ($00)

	MARCH	JUNE	SEPT	DEC
ASSETS				
CURRENT ASSETS:				
CASH	52,5	45,0	38,6	36,3
ACCOUNTS RECEIVABLE	6,0	8,0	8,0	10,0
INVENTORY	120,0	120,0	120,0	120,0
TOTAL CURRENT ASSETS	178,5	173,0	166,6	166,3
FIXED ASSETS:				
MACHINERY & EQUIPMENT	30,0	30,0	30,0	30,0
FURNITURE & FIXTURES	10,0	10,0	10,0	10,0
TOTAL FIXED ASSETS	40,0	40,0	40,0	40,0
ACCUMULATED DEPRECIATION	8,2	10,9	13,6	16,3
NET FIXED ASSETS	31,8	29,1	26,4	23,7
TOTAL ASSETS	210,3	202,1	193,0	190,0
LIABILITIES & STKHLDRS EQUITY				
CURRENT LIABILITIES:				
ACCOUNTS PAYABLE	30,0	30,0	30,0	30,0
PAYROLL TAXES PAYABLE	1,0	1,0	1,0	1,0
TOTAL CURRENT LIABILITIES	31,0	31,0	31,0	31,0
LONG-TERM LIABILITIES:				
LEASES PAYABLE	20,0	19,0	18,0	17,0
BANK LOAN PAYABLE	150,0	135,0	120,0	105,0
STOCKHOLDERS EQUITY:				
COMMON STOCK	10,0	10,0	10,0	10,0
PRIOR YEAR PROFIT (LOSS)	5,0	5,0	5,0	5,0
CURRENT YEAR PROFIT (LOSS)	-5,7	2,1	9,0	22,0
TOTAL EQUITY	9,3	17,1	24,0	37,0
TOTAL LIABILITIES & S/E	210,3	202,1	193,0	190,0

HOME IMPROVEMENTS, INC.
CASH FLOW STATEMENT
YEAR ONE - 1992
Rounded to Hundreds ($00)

	MARCH	JUNE	SEPT	DEC	YEAR ONE
NET INCOME (LOSS)	-5,7	7,8	6,9	13,0	22,0
SOURCE:					
DEPRECIATION	2,7	2,7	2,7	2,7	10,8
USE:					
PURCHASE—PROP & EQUIP	,0	,0	,0	,0	,0
SOURCE (USE) FROM OPERATIONS	-3,0	10,5	9,6	15,7	32,8
(INCREASE) DECREASE:					
ACCOUNTS RECEIVABLE	-2,0	-2,0	,0	-2,0	-6,0
INVENTORY	-95,0	,0	,0	,0	-95,0
INCREASE (DECREASE):					
ACCOUNTS PAYABLE	-20,0	,0	,0	,0	-20,0
PAYROLL TAXES PAYABLE	,0	,0	,0	,0	,0
LEASES PAYABLE	,0	-1,0	-1,0	-1,0	-3,0
(INCREASE) DECREASE:					
CASH	-30,0	7,5	6,4	2,3	-13,8
DISTRIBUTION TO STOCKHOLDERS	,0	,0	,0	,0	,0
CHANGE IN LOAN BALANCE	-150,0	15,0	15,0	15,0	-105,0
BALANCE BEGINNING OF QTR	,0	150,0	135,0	120,0	,0
LOAN BALANCE END OF QTR	150,0	135,0	120,0	105,0	105,0

125

HOME IMPROVEMENTS, INC.
PROFIT & LOSS STATEMENT
YEAR TWO - 1993
Rounded to Hundreds ($00)

	1	2	3	4	5	6	7	8	9	10	11	12	YEAR ONE
SALES	70,0	70,0	70,0	80,0	80,0	80,0	100,0	100,0	100,0	110,0	110,0	110,0	1080,0
COGS—MATERIALS	14,0	14,0	14,0	16,0	16,0	16,0	20,0	20,0	20,0	22,0	22,0	22,0	216,0
LABOR	9,1	9,1	9,1	10,4	10,4	10,4	13,0	13,0	13,0	14,3	14,3	14,3	140,4
TOTAL COGS	23,1	23,1	23,1	26,4	26,4	26,4	33,0	33,0	33,0	36,3	36,3	36,3	356,4
GROSS PROFIT/MARGIN	46,9	46,9	46,9	53,6	53,6	53,6	67,0	67,0	67,0	73,7	73,7	73,7	723,6
SELLING—COMMISSIONS	7,0	7,0	7,0	8,0	8,0	8,0	10,0	10,0	10,0	11,0	11,0	11,0	108,0
ADVERTISING	10,5	10,5	10,5	12,0	12,0	12,0	15,0	15,0	15,0	16,5	16,5	16,5	162,0
TOTAL SELLING	17,5	17,5	17,5	20,0	20,0	20,0	25,0	25,0	25,0	27,5	27,5	27,5	270,0
PROFIT BEFORE G&A	29,4	29,4	29,4	33,6	33,6	33,6	42,0	42,0	42,0	46,2	46,2	46,2	453,6
TOTAL G&A (SCHEDULE)	26,5	26,5	26,5	26,5	26,5	26,5	28,7	28,7	28,7	28,7	28,7	28,7	331,2
PROFIT (LOSS) BEFORE TAX	2,9	2,9	2,9	7,1	7,1	13,3	13,3	13,3	13,3	17,5	17,5	17,5	122,4
ESTIMATED INCOME TAX													43,4
PROFIT AFTER TAX													79,0

HOME IMPROVEMENTS, INC.
GENERAL & ADMINISTRATIVE EXPENSE
YEAR TWO - 1993
Rounded to Hundreds ($00)

	1	2	3	4	5	6	7	8	9	10	11	12	YEAR TWO
SALARIES—EMPLOYEES	14,4	14,4	14,4	14,4	14,4	14,4	16,0	16,0	16,0	16,0	16,0	16,0	182,4
SALARIES—OFFICERS	5,0	5,0	5,0	5,0	5,0	5,0	5,0	5,0	5,0	5,0	5,0	5,0	60,0
PAYROLL TAXES/BENEFITS	1,6	1,6	1,6	1,6	1,6	1,6	1,7	1,7	1,7	1,7	1,7	1,7	19,8
VEHICLE EXPENSE	,4	,4	,4	,4	,4	,4	,4	,4	,4	,4	,4	,4	4,8
INSURANCE	,3	,3	,3	,3	,3	,3	,3	,3	,3	,3	,3	,3	3,6
LEGAL & ACCOUNTING	,3	,3	,3	,3	,3	,3	,3	,3	,3	,3	,3	,3	3,6
GENERAL OFFICE EXP	,2	,2	,2	,2	,2	,2	,3	,3	,3	,3	,3	,3	3,0
POSTAGE	,2	,2	,2	,2	,2	,2	,3	,3	,3	,3	,3	,3	3,0
OFFICE SUPPLIES	,3	,3	,3	,3	,3	,3	,3	,3	,3	,3	,3	,3	3,0
TELEPHONE	,3	,3	,3	,3	,3	,3	,4	,4	,4	,4	,4	,4	4,2
RENT	,8	,8	,8	,8	,8	,8	1,0	1,0	1,0	1,0	1,0	1,0	10,8
UTILITIES	,8	,8	,8	,8	,8	,8	,8	,8	,8	,8	,8	,8	9,6
DEPRECIATION	,3	,3	,3	,3	,3	,3	,3	,3	,3	,3	,3	,3	3,6
TRAVEL	1,2	1,2	1,2	1,2	1,2	1,2	1,2	1,2	1,2	1,2	1,2	1,2	14,4
ENTERTAINMENT	,3	,3	,3	,3	,3	,3	,3	,3	,3	,3	,3	,3	3,6
MISCELLANEOUS	,2	,2	,2	,2	,2	,2	,2	,2	,2	,2	,2	,2	2,4
TOTAL G&A EXPENSE	26,5	26,5	26,5	26,5	26,5	26,5	28,7	28,7	28,7	28,7	28,7	28,7	331,2

HOME IMPROVEMENTS, INC.
QUARTERLY BALANCE SHEET
YEAR TWO - 1993
Rounded to Hundreds ($00)

	MARCH	JUNE	SEPT	DEC
ASSETS				
CURRENT ASSETS:				
CASH	6,2	13,1	16,7	11,4
ACCOUNTS RECEIVABLE	14,0	16,0	20,0	22,0
INVENTORY	130,0	130,0	150,0	150,0
TOTAL CURRENT ASSETS	150,2	159,1	186,7	183,4
FIXED ASSETS:				
MACHINERY & EQUIPMENT	50,0	50,0	50,0	50,0
FURNITURE & FIXTURES	20,0	20,0	20,0	20,0
TOTAL FIXED ASSETS	70,0	70,0	70,0	70,0
ACCUMULATED DEPRECIATION	19,9	23,5	27,1	30,7
NET FIXED ASSETS	50,1	46,5	42,9	39,3
TOTAL ASSETS	200,3	205,6	229,6	222,7
LIABILITIES & STKHLDRS EQUITY				
CURRENT LIABILITIES:				
ACCOUNTS PAYABLE	37,0	37,0	37,0	37,0
PAYROLL TAXES PAYABLE	1,6	1,6	1,7	1,7
TOTAL CURRENT LIABILITIES	38,6	38,6	38,7	38,7
LONG-TERM LIABILITIES:				
LEASES PAYABLE	26,0	25,0	24,0	23,0
BANK LOAN PAYABLE	90,0	75,0	60,0	45,0
STOCKHOLDERS EQUITY:				
COMMON STOCK	10,0	10,0	10,0	10,0
PRIOR YEAR PROFIT (LOSS)	27,0	27,0	27,0	27,0
CURRENT YEAR PROFIT (LOSS)	8,7	30,0	69,9	79,0
TOTAL EQUITY	45,7	67,0	106,9	116,0
TOTAL LIABILITIES & S/E	200,3	205,6	229,6	222,7

HOME IMPROVEMENTS, INC.
CASH FLOW STATEMENT
YEAR TWO - 1993
Rounded to Hundreds ($00)

	MARCH	JUNE	SEPT	DEC	YEAR TWO
NET INCOME (LOSS)	8,7	21,3	39,9	9,1	79,0
SOURCE:					
DEPRECIATION	3,6	3,6	3,6	3,6	14,4
USE:					
PURCHASE—PROP & EQUIP	30,0	,0	,0	,0	30,0
SOURCE (USE) FROM OPERATIONS	-17,7	24,9	43,5	12,7	63,4
(INCREASE) DECREASE:					
ACCOUNTS RECEIVABLE	-4,0	-2,0	-4,0	-2,0	-12,0
INVENTORY	-10,0	,0	-20,0	,0	-30,0
INCREASE (DECREASE):					
ACCOUNTS PAYABLE	7,0	,0	,0	,0	7,0
PAYROLL TAXES PAYABLE	,6	,0	,1	,0	,7
LEASES PAYABLE	9,0	-1,0	-1,0	-1,0	6,0
(INCREASE) DECREASE:					
CASH	30,1	6,9	3,6	5,3	24,9
DISTRIBUTION TO STOCKHOLDERS	,0	,0	,0	,0	,0
CHANGE IN LOAN BALANCE	15,0	15,0	15,0	15,0	60,0
BALANCE BEGINNING OF QTR	105,0	90,0	75,0	60,0	105,0
LOAN BALANCE END OF QTR	90,0	75,0	60,0	45,0	45,0

HOME IMPROVEMENTS, INC.
PROFIT & LOSS STATEMENT
YEARS THREE TO TEN
Rounded to Thousands ($000)

	YEAR THREE	YEAR FOUR	YEAR FIVE	YEAR SIX	YEAR SEVEN	YEAR EIGHT	YEAR NINE	YEAR TEN
SALES	1,240	1,430	1,640	1,890	2,170	2,500	2,870	3,300
COGS—MATERIALS	260	300	350	410	470	550	640	740
LABOR	160	190	220	260	300	350	400	460
TOTAL COGS	420	490	570	670	770	900	1,040	1,200
GROSS PROFIT/MARGIN	820	940	1,070	1,220	1,400	1,600	1,830	2,100
SELLING—COMMISSIONS	124	143	164	189	217	250	287	330
ADVERTISING	186	215	246	283	325	375	430	495
TOTAL SELLING	310	358	410	472	542	625	717	825
PROFIT BEFORE G&A	510	582	660	748	858	975	1,113	1,275
TOTAL G&A (SCHEDULE)	477	505	521	550	565	593	611	640
PROFIT BEFORE TAX	33	77	139	198	293	382	502	635
ESTIMATED INCOME TAX	8	20	47	74	120	150	212	269
PROFIT AFTER TAX	25	57	92	124	173	232	290	366

HOME IMPROVEMENTS, INC.
GENERAL AND ADMINISTRATION EXPENSE
YEARS THREE TO TEN
Rounded to Thousands ($000)

	YEAR THREE	YEAR FOUR	YEAR FIVE	YEAR SIX	YEAR SEVEN	YEAR EIGHT	YEAR NINE	YEAR TEN
SALARIES—EMPLOYEES	288	294	300	308	316	324	334	344
SALARIES—OFFICERS	72	78	84	88	92	96	100	104
PAYROLL TAXES/BENEFITS	28	30	31	32	32	33	34	35
VEHICLE EXPENSE	6	7	7	8	8	9	9	10
INSURANCE	4	5	5	6	6	7	7	8
LEGAL & ACCOUNTING	6	7	7	8	8	9	9	10
GENERAL OFFICE EXP	4	5	5	6	6	7	7	8
POSTAGE	4	5	5	6	6	7	7	8
OFFICE SUPPLIES	5	6	6	7	7	8	8	9
TELEPHONE	12	13	13	14	14	15	15	16
RENT	14	14	14	16	16	17	17	17
UTILITIES	6	7	7	8	8	9	9	10
DEPRECIATION	17	20	23	26	29	32	35	38
TRAVEL	5	6	6	7	7	8	8	9
ENTERTAINMENT	3	4	4	5	5	6	6	7
MISCELLANEOUS	3	4	4	5	5	6	6	7
TOTAL G&A EXPENSE	477	505	521	550	565	593	611	640

HOME IMPROVEMENTS, INC.
BALANCE SHEET
YEARS THREE TO SIX
Rounded to Thousands ($000)

	YEAR THREE	YEAR FOUR	YEAR FIVE	YEAR SIX
ASSETS				
CURRENT ASSETS:				
CASH	24	71	126	121
ACCOUNTS RECEIVABLE	25	25	30	35
INVENTORY	150	170	200	220
TOTAL CURRENT ASSETS	199	266	356	376
FIXED ASSETS:				
MACHINERY & EQUIPMENT	70	90	110	130
FURNITURE & FIXTURES	30	40	50	60
TOTAL FIXED ASSETS	100	130	160	190
ACCUMULATED DEPRECIATION	48	68	91	117
NET FIXED ASSETS	52	62	69	73
TOTAL ASSETS:	251	328	425	449
LIABILITIES & STKHLDRS EQUITY				
CURRENT LIABILITIES:				
ACCOUNTS PAYABLE	65	65	75	80
PAYROLL TAXES PAYABLE	5	5	5	5
TOTAL CURRENT LIABILITIES	70	70	80	85
LONG-TERM LIABILITIES:				
LEASES PAYABLE	40	60	55	50
BANK LOAN PAYABLE	0	0	0	0
STOCKHOLDERS EQUITY:				
COMMON STOCK	10	10	10	10
PRIOR YEAR PROFIT	106	131	188	280
CURRENT YEAR PROFIT	25	57	92	124
DISTRIBUTION TO STOCKHOLDERS	0	0	0	-100
TOTAL EQUITY	141	198	290	314
TOTAL LIABILITIES & S/E	251	328	425	449

HOME IMPROVEMENTS, INC.
CASH FLOW STATEMENT
YEARS THREE TO SIX
Rounded to Thousands ($000)

	YEAR THREE	YEAR FOUR	YEAR FIVE	YEAR SIX
NET INCOME	25	57	92	124
SOURCE:				
DEPRECIATION	17	20	23	26
USE:				
PURCHASE—PROP & EQUIP	30	30	30	30
SOURCE (USE) FROM OPERATIONS	12	47	85	120
(INCREASE) DECREASE:				
ACCOUNTS RECEIVABLE	-3	0	-5	-5
INVENTORY	0	-20	-30	-20
INCREASE (DECREASE):				
ACCOUNTS PAYABLE	28	0	10	5
PAYROLL TAXES PAYABLE	4	0	0	0
LEASES PAYABLE	17	20	-5	-5
(INCREASE) DECREASE:				
CASH	-13	-47	-55	5
DISTRIBUTION TO STOCKHOLDERS	0	0	0	-100
CHANGE IN LOAN BALANCE	45	0	0	0
BALANCE BEGINNING OF QTR	45	0	0	0
LOAN BALANCE END OF QTR	0	0	0	0

133

HOME IMPROVEMENTS, INC.
BALANCE SHEET
YEARS SEVEN TO TEN
Rounded to Thousands ($000)

	YEAR SEVEN	YEAR EIGHT	YEAR NINE	YEAR TEN
ASSETS				
CURRENT ASSETS:				
CASH	163	182	197	186
ACCOUNTS RECEIVABLE	40	45	50	60
INVENTORY	240	250	280	300
TOTAL CURRENT ASSETS	443	477	527	546
FIXED ASSETS:				
MACHINERY & EQUIPMENT	150	170	190	210
FURNITURE & FIXTURES	70	80	90	100
TOTAL FIXED ASSETS	220	250	280	310
ACCUMULATED DEPRECIATION	146	178	213	251
NET FIXED ASSETS	74	72	67	59
TOTAL ASSETS:	517	549	594	605
LIABILITIES & STKHLDRS EQUITY				
CURRENT LIABILITIES:				
ACCOUNTS PAYABLE	80	85	95	95
PAYROLL TAXES PAYABLE	5	5	5	5
TOTAL CURRENT LIABILITIES	85	90	100	100
LONG-TERM LIABILITIES:				
LEASES PAYABLE	45	40	35	30
BANK LOAN PAYABLE	0	0	0	0
STOCKHOLDERS EQUITY:				
COMMON STOCK	10	10	10	10
PRIOR YEAR PROFIT	304	377	409	449
CURRENT YEAR PROFIT	173	232	290	366
DISTRIBUTION TO STOCKHOLDERS	-100	-200	-250	-350
TOTAL EQUITY	387	419	459	475
TOTAL LIABILITIES & S/E	517	549	594	605

HOME IMPROVEMENTS, INC.
CASH FLOW STATEMENT
YEARS SEVEN TO TEN
Rounded to Thousands ($000)

	YEAR SEVEN	YEAR EIGHT	YEAR NINE	YEAR TEN
NET INCOME	173	232	290	366
SOURCE: DEPRECIATION	29	32	35	38
USE: PURCHASE—PROP & EQUIP	30	30	30	30
SOURCE (USE) FROM OPERATIONS	172	234	295	374
(INCREASE) DECREASE:				
ACCOUNTS RECEIVABLE	-5	-5	-5	-10
INVENTORY	-20	-10	-30	-20
INCREASE (DECREASE):				
ACCOUNTS PAYABLE	0	5	10	0
PAYROLL TAXES PAYABLE	0	0	0	0
LEASES PAYABLE	-5	-5	-5	-5
(INCREASE) DECREASE:				
CASH	-42	-19	-15	11
DISTRIBUTION TO STOCKHOLDERS	-100	-200	-250	-350
CHANGE IN LOAN BALANCE	0	0	0	0
BALANCE BEGINNING OF QTR	0	0	0	0
LOAN BALANCE END OF QTR	0	0	0	0

Glossary

ACCOUNTS PAYABLE. The monies owed to suppliers of goods and services to the business.

ACCOUNTS RECEIVABLE. The monies that are owed the business from the sales of goods and services.

ACCRUAL BASIS ACCOUNTING. It records the sale, expense or other event when it actually occurs, rather when cash changes hands. It is not the actual receipt of payment that is important, but the "right" to receive it. The sales or costs are said to be "accrued."

ADMINISTRATIVE EXPENSE. Such expenses as salaries, stationery, postage, office supplies, telephone, depreciation of office equipment, and rent.

AMORTIZATION. The gradual payment of a debt through a schedule of payments or the process of writing off an intangible asset against expenses over the period of its economic useful life.

BACK-END SELLING. Selling additional products and services to existing customers that have previously purchased from you at an earlier date.

BAD DEBT. Debts to the business that are either uncollectible or likely to be uncollectible.

BALANCE SHEET. Describes the assets, liabilities and net worth of the company on some fixed day.

BOARD OF DIRECTORS. A group of individuals elected by the stock holders, who as a body, manage the corporation.

BREAK-EVEN ANALYSIS. The method of determining the exact point at which the business neither makes a loss nor makes a profit.

BUDGETING. The planning and coordination of revenues and expenses over a specific period of time.

BUSINESS PLAN. A written document that describes the business, its objectives, strategies, operating plans, environment and marketing strategies, together with a financial forecast. It is the road map for managing the business.

BUSINESS RECEIPTS. Sales and/or receipts from the operations of the business.

CAPITAL. The general term for monies invested into a business enterprise.

CAPITAL BUDGET. A plan that describes the purchase of capital items such as equipment, buildings, leasehold improvements, and vehicles.

CASH BASIS ACCOUNTING. An accounting system where the sale or expense is recorded only when the transfer of cash occurs.

CASH FLOW ANALYSIS. The systematic charting of the sources and uses of cash in a business.

COLLATERAL. Personal or business assets that a borrower assigns to the lender to help ensure debt payment.

CONVERTIBLE LOAN. A loan to the business whereby the lender has the option of repayment of the loan or taking part ownership of the business.

CORPORATION. An organization formed under a state statute for the purpose of carrying on an enterprise in such a way as to make the enterprise distinct from the persons who control it.

COST OF GOODS AND SERVICES SOLD. Cost directly associated with making or providing the goods or services. Usually include raw material costs, building costs, machine costs, and other variable overhead.

CURRENT ASSETS. Cash, marketable securities, accounts receivables, and inventory owned by the business that can be liquidated quickly.

CURRENT LIABILITIES. Debts that must be met within a relatively short time, usually within one year, such as short term loans, accounts payable, wages payable, and accrued taxes.

CUSTOMER PROFILE. Description of the customer, including type, characteristics and habits.

CYCLICALITY. The variations in business revenue related to economic conditions and seasonality.

DEBT FINANCING. The use of borrowed money to finance a business. The loan is repaid in the form of principle and interest; the lender does not receive part ownership of the business.

DEMOGRAPHICS. Profiling the customers by Age, Sex, Family Size, Income, Occupation, Education, Religion, Culture and Social Class.

DEPRECIATION. The process of expensing the decreased value of a fixed asset over it's useful life.

DIRECT LABOR. Labor costs directly associated with production or contract work.

DOUBLE ENTRY BOOKKEEPING. A bookkeeping method where transactions are first entered in a journal or log, then posted to ledger accounts to show income, expenses, assets, liabilities and net worth. Each account classification allows for the recording of debits and credits.

EQUITY. The net value of assets minus liabilities; also known as net worth.

EQUITY FINANCING. The securing of monies from an investor in which the investor becomes part owner of the business.

EXIT PROGRAM. The ability of an investor to exit a venture by turning his investment into cash or other easily traded instrument.

EXPORTING. Selling products and services outside of a company's general geographical area; generally associated with shipping goods into foreign countries.

FISCAL YEAR. The year end (usually consists of a twelve month period), established by a business for accounting, planning, and tax purposes.

FINANCIAL REPORTS. Reports that show the financial status of a company at a given time.

FINANCIAL STATEMENT. A written presentation of financial data prepared from the accounting records. Statements include a Balance Sheet, Income Statement (or profit and loss statement), and Cash Flow Statement.

FIRST IN—FIRST OUT (FIFO). A method of valuing inventory. Assumes that the goods first acquired are the goods first sold. It is the method most commonly used, largely because it conforms to the physical flow of the inventory.

FIXED ASSET. Equipment, Buildings, Machinery, Vehicles, and Leasehold Improvements that are used in the business.

FIXED COSTS. Those business costs that do not vary when sales volume changes.

FORECASTING. The systematic calculation of all reasonable probabilities about the business future.

FRANCHISE. A business that is contractually bound to operate on another company's concept and operating principles.

GENERAL AND ADMINISTRATIVE EXPENSES. Expenses that are directly associated with the management of the business and not with making or selling the product or service.

GOODWILL. An intangible asset related to the perceived value of the business's assets.

IMPORTING. Buying products and services from individuals or companies outside of the general geographical area; usually associated with bringing goods in from foreign countries.

INCOME STATEMENT. A standard accounting format for determining the profit and loss of a business; usually yearly, quarterly or monthly.

INDUSTRY LIFE CYCLE. The cycle of events that occur during a business lifetime; including introductory stage, growth stage, maturity stage, and decline stage.

INSIDE SALES FORCE. Those personnel who are in direct contact with customers, but do not leave their place of work in the performance of their duties.

INTANGIBLE ASSET. Assets that do not have a physical presence, but have value, such as: Goodwill, Trademarks, Patents, Copyrights, Formulas, Franchises, Brands, Customer Lists, and Mailing Lists.

INTEREST. The amount paid on borrowed money.

INTERIM FINANCING. Acquisition of funds for a short term when it is planned that by the end of that period, necessary financing of a longer term will be provided.

INVENTORY. Items that have been produced or purchased and will ultimately be sold; includes raw material inventory, work in progress inventory, and finished goods inventory.

INVENTORY FINANCING. The process of obtaining needed capital for a business by borrowing money with inventory used as collateral; or, as in the case of a TRADE ACCEPTANCE, a method used for financing the purchase of inventories.

JOINT VENTURE. Partnership between two or more businesses to accomplish some task or business.

LAST-IN-FIRST OUT (LIFO). A method of valuing inventory. Assumes that the units sold are those most recently acquired and that the units on hand are those first acquired.

LEVERAGE. The use of credit/borrowing to increase the ability to conduct business.

LINE OF CREDIT. An advance commitment by a bank to lend up to the amount indicated.

LIQUIDITY. The amount of cash that can be generated in a short time from the sale of assets.

MANAGEMENT CONSULTANT. A specialist outside a business who advises the business on management matters. Professional consultants have three basic advantages over company officers and employees:

1. They bring in a point of view attained by experience with many enterprises; they can see things in proper perspective.

2. Their approach to problems is generally impartial, but it is advisable for management, when retaining a consultant, to emphasize that a predetermined result is not being sought.

3. Since such investigations are the consultant's operations, efforts are more concentrated on your investigation.

MARKET. A clearly defined group of people, area, or group of things that can be classified together as having some commonality.

MARKET ANALYSIS. Process of determining the characteristics of the market and the measurement of its capacity to buy products and services.

MARKETING. The act of identifying, informing, persuading, and satisfying the needs of customers.

MARKETING MIX. The array of marketing methods used to sell customers; includes product lines, product pricing, product promotion, and product distribution.

MARKETING PLAN. The combination of a Market Analysis and Marketing Strategies that defines who your competitors and customers are, and how you will promote your business to successfully obtain and maintain the customers' business.

MARKET RESEARCH. The act of uncovering information about a particular market. The information typically relates to the type of customers in that market, their buying habits, unfilled needs, and product or service information.

MARKET SEGMENTS. The logical breakdown and grouping of customers or customer needs or products.

MARKET SHARE. The sales of your business divided by the total sales of your industry for either your local market or national or international market. Usually expressed as a percentage.

NET PROFIT AFTER TAXES. Net profit before taxes less federal, state or local income or franchise taxes.

NET PROFIT BEFORE TAXES. Net sales or total receipts less all expenses, including interest.

NET SALES. Total sales less discounts, returned goods, and pricing allowances.

NET WORTH. The net value of assets minus liabilities.

NET WORTH OF A CUSTOMER. A calculated formula used to indicate the dollar value of a customer's patronage every time he/she buys from you.

NOTES PAYABLE. An account in the liability section of the general ledger showing the liability for promissory notes incurred by the business.

NOTES RECEIVABLE. An account in the asset section of the general ledger showing the amount of negotiable promissory notes received from customers in payment for goods sold and delivered.

OPERATING EXPENSES. Those expenses of the business that are not directly associated with the making or providing of the goods or services. They usually include administrative, technical and selling expenses.

CPERATIONAL PLAN. The detailed action plan you will take to implement strategies and reach desired goals. It covers the near term action items, up to one, two or three years in the future.

OPERATIONS. The daily, weekly or monthly activities of the business.

OUTSIDE SALES FORCE. Personnel who perform the selling function and meet with customers either at the customers location or outside the salesperson's business office.

PARTNERSHIP. The Uniform Partnership Act defines the arrangement as an "association of two or more persons to carry-on as co-owners of a business for profit."

PATENT. An exclusive right, granted by the federal government, to make, use, and sell an invention for a fixed period of time.

PREFERRED STOCK. Stock that is given a preference over other forms of stock within the same corporation, primarily with respect to dividend payments.

PRO FORMA. A projection of future (often financial) activity.

PROJECTED FINANCIALS. An estimation of future financial earnings and expenses.

PROPRIETORSHIP, SOLE. An individual owner of a business who has not incorporated, nor has a recognized partner. The owner is liable for all the debts of the business to the full extent of his or her property.

PUBLIC OFFERING. When a business goes into the financial market to secure capital financing by offering shares or stock in the company to the public.

QUICK RATIO. Cash plus Accounts Receivable divided by Current Liabilities.

REORGANIZATION. A process involving a recasting of corporate capital structure which the corporation may be compelled to undergo because of either imminent or immediate insolvency.

RETAINED EARNINGS. Net profit after taxes that is retained in the business as working capital and not paid out as dividends to stockholders.

RETURN ON EQUITY. Profit on the total Equity in the company.

RETURN ON GROSS OPERATING ASSETS. Profit on the total assets used in the business.

RETURN ON INVESTMENT, ROI. Profit on the invested capital.

REVENUES. Used interchangeably with Sales. Often used for businesses that do not physically sell something, such as rental companies, contracting businesses, etc.

SECURITIES AND EXCHANGE COMMISSION. Government body that is chartered to maintain order and rules of the stock and securities exchanges.

SELLING EXPENSES. Expenses incurred in selling or distributing a product or service.

SMALL BUSINESS ADMINISTRATION (SBA). An independent agency of the Federal Government, under the general direction and supervision of the President. The SBA is authorized to furnish credit either as a maker of a direct loan, or as a guarantor in part of a loan made by a bank to a business.

STRATEGIC OPPORTUNITY. An opportunity or goal that will change the basic thrust or strategies of the business.

STRATEGY. The basic method used to reach the goal.

TRADE RECEIVABLES. See Accounts Receivable.

TRADE PAYABLES. See Accounts Payable.

UNEMPLOYMENT INSURANCE. A Federal-state system that provides temporary income for workers, when they are unemployed, due to circumstances beyond their control.

UNIQUE SELLING ADVANTAGE (USA). The essential appeal a business owner develops to share with staff members and customers. It is all the unique reasons why customers should buy from your company, all stated in one crisp, easy-to-understand paragraph.

UNSECURED LOAN. A loan made with no actual collateral or security posted to guarantee payment of the loan.

VARIABLE COST. Costs that vary directly with sales. These include raw material costs, certain utility costs, labor, sales commissions, and advertising.

VARIANCES. An accounting term for the difference between what was forecast and what actually happened.

VENTURE CAPITAL. A pool of investment dollars made by private investors who provide counsel designed to enhance the investment, and who usually will require controlling or a major interest of the company.

VERTICAL DISINTEGRATION. The breaking up of manufacturing and supply operations into discrete smaller units that are completely separate entities. Often independently owned.

WORKING CAPITAL. Current Assets less Current Liabilities.

Small Business Best-Sellers!

The Complete Book of Business Plans by Joseph Covello and Brian Hazelgren
With 11 actual plans to guide you, this book will show you how to write a powerful and effective business plan. Eliminate the frustration of starting a new business, or even get cash out of and existing business, by learning the critical elements required by investors, lenders, and buyers.
"A must-have book for every business!"
  —R. N. Nunley, President, Protecto Rolling Shutters, Inc.
             328 pages, ISBN 0-942061-41-1 (paperback), $19.95

Mancuso's Small Business Resource Guide by Joseph R. Mancuso
The ultimate directory of small business information, with complete information on every resource your business must have, including venture capital, government assistance, franchising, on-line services, home-based businesses, and much more.
"This directory will prove a great time saver, providing the names, addresses and phone numbers that will get you started on the road to self-employment."
  —*Opportunity Magazine*
             208 pages, ISBN 1-57071-066-X (paperback), $9.95

Great Idea! Now What? by Howard Bronson and Peter Lange
Turn your idea, invention or business concept into a moneymaking success with a complete process for developing, testing, producing and marketing your great idea.
—Recommended by *Entrepreneur Magazine*
"Must reading!"
  —*Houston Post*
"One of the best how-to marketing books ever written!"
  —*CNBC, Smart Money*
             224 pages, ISBN 1-57071-039-2 (paperback), $9.95

The Small Business Survival Guide by Robert E. Fleury
Learn to manage your cash, profits and taxes. Plus, No Entry Accounting—an easy way of doing and understanding your own accounting without double entry book-keeping.
"Innovative ways of managing cash flow and accounting problems."
  —Jane Applegate, Syndicated Columnist, *Los Angeles Times*
"One of the 75 best resources for starting a company."
  —*Inc. Magazine*
             256 pages, ISBN 1-57071-045-2 (paperback), $17.95

These best-selling books are all available at your local bookstore or call Sourcebooks at 708-961-3900. Get a copy of our catalog by writing or faxing:

Sourcebooks, Inc.
P. O. Box 372
Naperville, IL 60566
(708) 961-3900
FAX: (708) 961-2168